MARY ANNE LAPORTE

STEP CRAZY

THE RAW EMOTIONS
OF A STEP FAMILY

Copyright © 2017 by Mary Anne LaPorte. All rights reserved. This book may not be reproduced or stored in whole or in part by any means without the written permission of the author except for brief quotations for the purpose of review.

17 15

ISBN: 978-1-943258-98-7
　　　978-1-943258-39-0

Published by Warren Publishing, Inc.
Charlotte, NC
www.warrenpublishing.net
Printed in the United States

Contents

Introduction	6
Chapter 1: *The Wedding*	9
Chapter 2: *Tom*	21
Chapter 3: *After the Divorce*	30
Chapter 4: *Josie*	33
Chapter 5: *The Early Years Of Our Marriage*	46
Chapter 6: *Creating My Own Environment*	52
Chapter 7: *The Arrival of James*	79
Chapter 8: *The Teen Years: Andrew and Sarah*	82
Chapter 9: *Sarah*	85
Chapter 10: *James, My Biological Son, Why Do I Describe Him That Way?*	89
Chapter 11: *Step Friends*	94
Chapter 12: *Holidays*	97
Chapter 13: *That is not your seat! Don't touch my things! She is not my sister! He is not my brother! I hate you!*	99
Chapter 14: *It's Our Turn*	101

DEDICATION

*I dedicate this book to my husband of 30 years,
who step-parented with me every step of the way. We questioned
our parenting skills at least once a day, and talked about the children,
biological and step, almost every night. We are proud of all our
children and pray that their marriages survive struggles and
challenges they might meet along the way. If in fact, they should
find themselves in a step-parenting situation someday, I truly
hope they seek counseling and work together to create a
healthy balance for their marriage and the children.*

Acknowledgments

I would like to thank my family and friends for their continued support and patience throughout the writing of this book. A big thanks to my neighbor, Jane Irene Kelly, Freelance Writer/Editor, who was helpful and offered her guidance and suggestions. And last but not least, Thank you Warren Publishing, for making my dream come true. Writing this book has been a wonderful experience because you took the anxiety away by being so supportive and professional. I am very grateful to have worked with your team.

Introduction

I want to explain the emotional demeanor throughout this book to my readers. I am a stepparent and have experienced many different feelings and emotions while raising our children, step and biological. Although this book is all fiction and none of the events actually happened, the feelings described and emotions displayed are not rare, and many stepparents have probably realized the same in their step situations.

Many of these feelings and emotions are never verbalized, but are internalized and can affect the relationship in years to come for all involved. I think we, as stepparents, harbor our true emotions because we feel that expressing them makes us look bad as parents. We lock them away somewhere and think it is our fault that our family is struggling to get along. If you are a biological parent and NOT a stepparent, you may think ill of this book or, at the very least, have a difficult time understanding what stepparents go through. The feelings are real, and I hope I can explain the reason for these feelings and how hard it is to process them without some sort of counseling.

The stepchild goes through the same emotional turmoil. It is a challenging situation for all. It is a step crazy environment!

I have intentionally exaggerated these emotions, because when we're feeling them and they are internalized, they do become exaggerated in the "step mind," so to speak. If we could step back, take a look at what is happening from a distance, and receive some counseling, our step lives would be more peaceful.

I hope you enjoy reading this book. My intent is to let you know that if you are a stepparent and have some crazy feelings and emotions, you are not alone. Your marriage can survive this.

Step Crazy

You're not my mom!
You're not my dad!
I don't have to listen to you!
We never did it this way!

I have come to realize that the hardest job on earth is living in the "step" environment. It not only presents a physical challenge, balancing all the activities, remembering to invite everyone to all those family events, cooking for three children instead of one, attending PTA meetings, etc. It is also an emotional challenge — a bit like being thrown into shark-infested waters, albeit with a positive attitude, and being expected to swim happily.

Any family that has gone through stepparenting knows exactly what I am talking about!

I swore it would not happen to us, but guess what…

Chapter One

The Wedding
August 11, 2014

My husband Tom was 61 years old, and I was 56. In reality, we felt at least 10 years older. Raising a stepfamily seemed like it had taken years off our lives. As a little girl, I envisioned getting married to a man and starting a family together, but I never even considered the thought that I would marry someone who already had a child, let alone two children.

But here we were, years later, and we had raised our blended family. Step and biological, our children were now grown up and leaving home. The oldest was getting married on the day these next events unfolded.

"Josie, it's time for us to leave," shouted Tom.

"I'm ready," I responded, as I walked down the stairs.

Tom turned to me and said, "Jo, did you ever think we would get to this point in our married life? I mean, with Andrew getting married today, Sarah in her own apartment and James nearly graduated from college?"

"You're right, Tom. There were times I didn't think our marriage would survive the children." We laughed as we hugged, then Tom looked at me and held my face with his strong, gentle hands and said, "I love you, Jo, and it was not always easy, but it was worth it every step of the way."

He kissed me so tenderly, and I knew he still loved me. I thought, not many couples still have this passionate love, these passionate feelings, after 25 years. I am a lucky woman. I still feel that way today. I know Tom and I have something special.

"Well, we don't want to be late," he said. "Let's go see our son get married."

Oh, what a nice touch, I thought. He called him "our" son. I have always felt he really is my son, and Sarah really is my daughter. What could a day like that bring, other than happy times, memories, and love?

Andrew was already at the church, and James, our biological son and Andrew's best man, was with him. Sarah was getting dressed at her mother's.

Andrew, Sarah, and James were as close as any siblings could be. James idolized his brother and he was always very protective of Sarah, even though he was younger than her.

We arrived at the church a little early and waited for our instructions. As we waited, I start to think about all the years spent raising these three children.

I hardly remember some of the early years. They flew by in such emotional turmoil. There were many good times, and the bad times… Well, we didn't view them as bad times. We just tried to handle each situation as it came along, right or wrong. I am proud of how all three children have grown to be independent adults. I'm not really sure how we did that. As with any family, step or not, there are times when you struggle. There was never a minute to stop, think, and/or analyze the situation. Situations just happened.

I thought about the wedding situation, and wondered how we got to this point. I was feeling many emotions as a stepparent. That very day, my stepson Andrew was marrying Amy, the love of his life, and he had to share it with his stepmom.

I remember trying to lie low and let the biological parents shine, and it was hard. You see, I pretty much raised Andrew. I loved him and wanted to be a part of that day. But, I had to understand that it was not my privilege to be important or even proud. I could be proud after his mom and dad, but I even had to be careful when and where I told him I was proud. It was so important not to take the limelight away from his biological mother.

Oh, too much thought goes into step-parenting — so much more than biological parenting.

Andrew walked by us to talk to the wedding planner on the other side of the room. He acknowledged his father, but not me. Tom looked at me and said, "I am sorry, Jo."

"No worries, Tom. I am used to it now." I laughed a little as I thought, this can't be happening — not today.

So, there I was in a church, participating in a wedding where it was obvious that my stepson was uncomfortable having me there. Besides the nervousness of the whole wedding day event, Andrew had to make sure he didn't offend his mother, Alice, on his special day. Remember, she gave birth to him. And, as his mother had drummed into him, he should be loyal to her and no other. He didn't want his mother to feel uncomfortable at all, and I understood that. Andrew knew that if Alice observed him being too nice to me, she would be jealous. Then she would start to chastise him, and from there, the mood of the day would deteriorate.

No matter how childish I felt Andrew's mom was behaving, this was his wedding day, and I would do nothing to put a damper on it. I truly felt badly for Andrew that he had to have such pressure on him on the one day that should have been his to enjoy.

And it wasn't that Andrew didn't like me. He just wished things were different. He wanted his mom and his dad together on his special day.

I understood his feelings. I tried for many years to create an atmosphere that would nurture the children's "divorce demeanor," if you will, in a positive way. Sometimes it worked, and sometimes it didn't.

My stepson is 6 feet tall and very heavy, about 250 pounds. He has blond, curly hair that is always disheveled. Andrew is a presence when he walks into a room, not only because of his size, but because he speaks loudly and likes to be the center of attention. His fiancée, Amy, is average height, about 5'5", and a healthy weight. Amy has curly brown hair. She is very kind, and very much in love with Andrew. Amy tends to let Andrew be in the spotlight, which is a good thing, because that way they don't compete with each other.

They seemed to be a happy couple. Andrew and Amy did not date very long — about six months — so Amy was not quite up to par on the family dynamics. When Andrew wanted something, he got it. He wanted to marry Amy, so there they were.

It was mid-August and very hot. The church was air conditioned — somewhat. The wedding took place in Annapolis, MD, where my stepson lives. The reception was held about 10 miles from the church, at a boat club overlooking the bay. It was a beautiful setting.

The bay has always been special for Andrew. His mom and dad took him there a lot when he was very young, and then Andrew attended a private college near Annapolis. He met Amy after he graduated.

Amy went to a prestigious school in Washington, DC, and grew up south of Annapolis. They met at the docks, outside an ice cream shop one Saturday afternoon. Amy's family loved sailboats, and she had just walked out of the ice cream shop with a big peach ice cream cone. She sat on the benches near the dock to watch the sailboats in Ego Alley. That was the nickname for the area where the sailboats docked, if they were lucky enough to get a slip. It was right at the base of the town, in front of the fish market. The slips were always full and very expensive, even for a few hours. The boats that could afford to dock there were beautiful.

Andrew came out of the ice cream shop and sat on one of the benches overlooking Ego Alley. He was with a friend, watching the yachts that had slips there, and commented on one of the yachts.

"I think I could handle a 50-foot yacht. How many miles to the gallon do you think it gets?"

To his surprise, Amy answered, "Not many! That's why my family prefers a sailboat." To this day, they still argue over which is the best — sail or motor. The rest is history.

Most of my relatives would be attending the wedding, and the best part of the day for me would be spending time with my family. My brother James was retired from the military, and I was looking forward to seeing him. A few cousins would be attending, and it seemed like we only got to see each other at weddings and funerals.

The wedding planner made her entrance, with Andrew and his mother right behind her. I figured I must be doing something wrong, because they were heading toward me. I remember thinking, Is my dress okay? Do I have on the wrong color? Am I not holding my flowers correctly? I was sure they would find something, and I was relieved when they walked right by me.

My plan for the day was to fade into the background and Andrew could pretend he didn't notice me. I could handle that. I would keep quiet and stay out of everyone's way. My dress was subdued, my heels were low, and my makeup was minimal. I did not want to stand out.

When Andrew's mother and I are in the same room, Andrew always finds a way to insult me. It could be something as simple as a roll of his eyes when I say something, or sometimes it's a huff or a laugh if I do something he does not like. It's all for his mother, and I can't help but wonder, haven't we gotten past this point by now? He does not want his mother to think that he shares his love with me in any way. He has always felt it would hurt her if he showed me any attention. I try to ignore his reactions, but it hurts.

I have always known his loyalties lie with his mother, and I have told him over the years that I understand that and would not expect him to be any other way. Andrew loves his mother very much. Alice was never able to get over the fact that Andrew would have another mother in his life. She should have been encouraging him to be respectful to me all those years, but she was always so jealous of any time I spent with him. I have tried to understand and be the bigger person, because I love Andrew and I know it is important that he feel love from all of us.

I know Andrew cares for me as a special friend, but I don't believe he will ever love me the way he loves his mother or dad, and I cannot expect that. I just hope I have a special place in his heart. That is all I can ask for as a stepparent.

I do wish he could be polite to me when his mother is around. His reactions to me are like night and day. His mother definitely lays a guilt trip on him, and it works.

I remember wondering how Alice would react once Andrew and Amy were married for a few years. Would she be jealous of Amy? Maybe she would be happy for him and/or see less of us. Either option would be good for me!

The wedding was about to begin, and we were asked to go to a side room in the church as people started to arrive. Andrew, Alice, and the wedding planner were discussing procedure for the wedding. I felt badly for Sam, Alice's husband. As they walked away from him, they turned their backs to him and started to talk. They stood in a circle, talking softly, as if to keep what they were saying a secret. Tom and I were several feet away, talking about the beautiful day. Andrew called, "Hey, Dad, come here a minute, would you?" And just like that, it was my turn to be left standing alone. How silly that I even noticed.

Tom walked over and became part of their little circle, turning his back to me. It was evident that Andrew and his mother were saying, "We wish you weren't here," I remember thinking, how very rude it is to walk away from someone and leave them standing alone. Didn't I teach him better than that? How can people do this? I have never blatantly ignored anyone.

I could hear them talking about the procedure for walking down the aisle. This ought to be interesting.

Sam looked at me and walked over to talk.

"Sam," I said. "Don't you ever get tired of being excluded and treated so rudely?"

"Yes, I do," he said. "The thing is, Josie, Alice only does this around Andrew and Tom. It's like she can't let go." I have tried to discuss her behavior with her, and she just says, "Sam, you do not understand!"

Sam and I stood there, trying to make small talk and give the appearance that we were enjoying the day.

Sam finally said to me, "Hey, let's have a pact today. If we are left alone, let's find each other. At least we can be miserable together." I immediately relaxed, for the moment, and replied, "Sounds good to me!"

We laughed as we looked around and wondered aloud how this situation might look to others.

"Sam, we might be spending the whole evening together by the looks of things." Sam and I understand each other, because we are both the "other" parent. Sam is a nice man, and he seems to be a genuinely kind person. He owns the gourmet restaurant in town, which seems to do well, and I know he works very hard.

In stepfamilies at family functions, it is sometimes hard to know who to talk to if you are the stepparent. Will you talk to the ex-wife, the grandparents of the stepchildren, the ex-wife's husband — because he is an outsider, too — or friends?

Do you talk about the children, or do you just make small talk with whoever will listen? All these things come into play. How do we sort it out?

I waited to see if anyone would say something — anything — to us. Sam and I only stood there for 10 minutes or so, but it seemed like an hour. Nope, not one word. Usually, Tom would step back and leave room for me in his circle, and if he was talking to someone and I walked up, he would acknowledge I was there. I did not belong this time, could not give an opinion, and was not welcome to be a part of their discussion or even their space. I guess Andrew was proving his point about who his family was.

I said to Sam, "Let's go see what the church looks like." We walked out of the room, and no one noticed.

At that point, I made up my mind to just play the game and put in my time. I didn't have enough energy left to say what I REALLY thought about what was happening. It was a very special moment for Andrew and Amy, and I had to respect their day. I could not add anything to the conversation unless I was asked, and it really hurt. It was a very tough day for me.

I didn't deserve it, but I did understand what was happening there. I didn't agree with it, but I understood it. I knew Tom had to do whatever he could to be sure his son's wedding day was beautiful.

Today started out so well, I thought. What happened?

Okay, let's be honest here. How did I really feel?

The more I thought about the situation, the angrier I got.

I had way too much time to think about it, and I wished I had something to do, some way to help with this wedding. I needed to be busy.

I was standing in the back of the church, taking it all in, and when I look back to that day now, that picture elicits many emotions for me. All kinds of thoughts were going through my head. Why didn't I leave years ago? Can I take the aggravation anymore? I know my life has been shortened!

Why was I feeling like this? I looked at my husband's ex-wife, and she looked so young! I hated it. She had not had the stress I had; the stress of raising her children! I had to carry her stress! She had no stress lines, and she had time to work out every day at the gym. The only workouts I got were the ones driving our children to and from activities. I stood there thinking, if Alice had shared in some of the parenting activities, I might have had the time to go to the gym, go for a run…

I knew one stressor would be out of my daily routine after this wedding, and I thought maybe my life would calm down a little. I know it sounds like I didn't get along with my stepson, but it wasn't like that. It was just that the situation changed with every event, depending on who was in attendance.

Many stepfamilies might not admit this, but they are feeling it, I can tell you.

When I look back to the first few months after Tom and I were married, the kids seemed to like me. Whenever I gave them money or presents, they REALLY liked me.

So, the question sometimes becomes, How much money does it take for a stepchild to like their stepparent? This is not a joke. When I first married Tom, a friend of mine asked me this question, and I looked at her with disgust.

"Sandy, I am going to work hard at this and hopefully my stepchildren will come to love me," I replied. "I will treat them like my own children."

In retrospect, I have to agree with her. At times, it felt like money was the only thing that worked. I knew it was wrong to buy their love, but sometimes it seemed like there was no other option. Being a stepparent is NOT easy! Anyone who thinks it is should think again.

The wedding was getting ready to start, and the little circle had come out of the side room. The wedding planner was telling us to start walking down the aisle, and here was where the real problem of the day occurred. In fact, it was representative of the past 20 years, and was MAJOR to me!

I overheard Andrew reminding Tom, my husband, that he was supposed to walk down the aisle with Andrew's mom, and that he was also supposed to sit with her! And that Sam, Alice's husband, and I were to walk down the aisle together and sit behind them! Andrew said the only thing he wanted was for his father and mother to sit together on his wedding day.

The only thing he wanted, huh? Have you ever heard of anything so ridiculous? The exes sitting together! It was inappropriate, to say the least.

Oh well, anything to make Andrew happy. Right? Boy, was I bitter! I had to calm down before I gave them a reason to disrespect me.

Andrew made most of the decisions for the wedding, and seemed to be living in a fairy tale — one where his mother and father were still married.

I predicted Andrew would find a way to get his parents together at his wedding. I thought it might be in the wedding pictures, but I honestly did not think he would have them sit together in the church with their spouses sitting in the pew behind them.

I had discussed the possibility of this happening with Tom months ago, but Tom said I was overreacting. He felt Andrew would consider our feelings and recognize us, and his mom and Sam, as married couples. Tom had assured me that Andrew would be respectful and not put us in an uncomfortable situation.

Andrew displayed such determination in his decision to have his mother and father sit together in the pew. He was in tears as he talked to his father and told him, once again, how happy it would make him if he could see his mom and dad sitting together on his special day. He was 32 years old, but he was acting like he was eight.

Tom just walked away, and I thought, how many times have I seen that behavior? You know the one — not wanting to tell your child he is wrong, because then he will feel bad all over again because you got divorced!

The wedding planner moved Andrew and his groomsmen to the room in front of the church to prepare for their entrance. After Andrew left, Tom looked at me and saw my expression.

Did Andrew actually think that I was going to walk down the aisle and sit with Sam in the pew behind my husband instead of with my husband? Anything to make me uncomfortable! What about doing the right thing?

I could handle a step wedding with our exes. It was public. It was generic. It could be comfortable. We could all be civil. In fact, there were even times when I felt like I could be friends with Alice, but I would not pretend she and Tom were married again.

Oh, I was angry! I realized I'd better focus on walking down the aisle and sitting with Tom's ex-wife's new husband! How's that for a label?

I realized that in Andrew's mind, it was not about doing the right thing. It was about control! It was one more opportunity to have a power struggle and try to show that Sam and I were not part of his family.

Not part of his family? I bought all his school clothes, took him to baseball practice, attended parent-teacher conferences, cooked for him, cleaned for him...

Tom tried to talk to Andrew about the wedding procession, but Andrew was belligerent from the beginning, so Tom backed off. Of course, Alice would never say a word to Andrew. She wanted to walk down the aisle with Tom. What has that been about all these years? They divorced, and it was agreeable to both of them.

I was making myself more upset by the minute, and I just needed to focus on the wedding and get through the day! Who am I kidding? I needed to be sedated!

Please understand that this was not only about Tom's ex-wife controlling the situation through her son. It was about Tom wanting Andrew to feel emotionally safe.

Most of this started when Andrew was young, and it was not totally Andrew's fault. It was our fault also — Tom's, mine, Alice's, and Sam's.

When Tom and Alice argued and disciplined Andrew, Andrew knew they still loved him. Stepparents often have a harder time creating that sense of emotional wellbeing and unconditional love for a stepchild.

It is regrettable that we, as a family, never sought counseling. It would have been beneficial. Talking to children about their stepparent is hard. A neutral third party might have been able to help the child view the stepparent in a more positive light.

I was standing there thinking about all of this, and all these emotions were popping up. Weddings are emotional! Divorces are emotional!

Step relationships are emotional! No wonder I was a mess! It really is amazing what can go through a person's mind in just a few minutes. Every interaction could be analyzed, but what good would it do?

"Tom, I am sitting with you unless you want another divorce!" I said, in a tone that ensured he knew I meant it.

"Oh, honey," he said. "I will handle this."

So the big moment came, and we were walking down the aisle, Tom and Alice in front, Sam and I trailing behind.

Just when I thought Tom was not going to do anything about the seating arrangement, he surprised me. Alice turned into the front pew, Tom quickly went in the pew behind her, and I went with him. Sam caught on and smiled at me as he joined Alice. I don't think Alice was happy about that!

Tom gave me a quick squeeze around the shoulders and smiled at me. Sam looked very relieved to be able to sit with the love of his life. At least Alice still sat in the front row.

Andrew and Amy exchanged their vows and no one objected to the marriage. The minister introduced them as Mr. and Mrs. Andrew Walden, the guests applauded, the string quartet played, and the happy bride and groom walked down the aisle. We pulled it off!

If only the last 20 years could have been so simple.

As they walked out of the church, Andrew and Amy were totally into each other. Maybe this is what Andrew needed — someone else to focus on, instead of trying to prove to me that his father loves him more. Over the years, I tried to tell Andrew and Sarah that there is nothing stronger than a father and mother's love for their children. The effects of a divorce are very hard on young children. I truly hope this turns my relationship with Andrew around. Who knows? Stepfamilies can be very complicated!

It was a beautiful evening on the bay. There was a full moon over the water and the weather was perfect. Maybe the reception would go well. At least I would be able to sit with my family and have some good conversation. And I was hungry!

As we got to the reception area, I began to peruse the table seating, looking for our names. Then I realized that Andrew and Amy had Sam and Alice sitting with us at a separate table. How nice. Just the four of us — how cozy. We even get to sit with Tom's ex for dinner. How thoughtful of Andrew and Amy!

Tom and I walked to our table, and Tom tried to sit next to Sam. "Oh, no!" said Alice. "Boy-girl, boy-girl." She put her hand on Sam's shoulder and moved him beside me. Tom did not like that, but I think I made out in that deal. At least I didn't have to sit beside Alice.

The conversation was, well, forgettable!

Alice tried talking about Andrew growing up and her time together with Tom. So, I started in with my stories, talking and laughing, and Tom joined in with a few comments. Sam laughed a little also. I think we were all tired of Alice's remarks and her attempts to stake her claim on a relationship that had been done for 20 years.

I wondered if she and Sam argued when they got home. He must have been embarrassed and humiliated by her comments. It appeared that she had no respect for him, and that was so sad, because he seemed to be a nice man. Alice never talked about her marriage, nor did she even acknowledge that he was in her company. How rude!

Sam loved Alice; you could see it in his eyes when he looked at her. He knew Alice was jealous of me, yet he put up with her inappropriate behavior in stepfamily situations. Why? I still can't figure that out.

The sad thing was that all four of us did not like the way this played out, but no one said anything. The only ones who should have said something were Andrew's parents, but they didn't because they still felt guilty about their divorce.

I really think that not allowing their children to deal with the divorce created more anger and resentment as the years went on. Thoughts of why their parents could not or would not be together just festered in Andrew's and Sarah's minds.

Sarah was much younger than Andrew when their parents divorced, and our life with Sarah seemed normal to her. She was with us from a younger age, and Sarah and I developed a healthy respect for one another that forged our close relationship. It was great to see Sarah so happy on Andrew's wedding day. At the reception, Sarah came up to me and said, "You look pretty, Jo." And she gave me a hug. That was all I needed to make the rest of the day go well.

The dancing and festivities were kind of fun. Our three children, our son James, 24, Tom's daughter Sarah, 29, and Andrew and his bride, Amy, were having a great time.

Andrew, Amy, and the bridal party were all sitting together. I remember thinking, only a few more hours of this. I think I will make it. I have developed very broad shoulders over the years, and this hasn't really been that bad... We had a good meal, Tom and I danced, and we were happy to welcome our new daughter-in-law.

The evening was just about over, and Tom and I were exhausted. As I thought about the past 25 years, I tried to recall how our family developed into what it is today. In fact, I do this and have done this almost every night since I married Tom. I go over every situation in my head, hoping to improve on it somehow or some way the next day.

I tried my best. Treating my stepchildren like my own was my first mistake!

I should have stayed neutral, and made the biological parent do the parenting, make decisions, monitor homework, call the shots, correct the table manners, attend the PTA meetings, etc. Because, no matter how hard I tried, it was wrong in the eyes of my stepchildren. If they were upset because I asked them to do something they did not want to do, or because I corrected them in some way, it was wrong in the eyes of my husband. I couldn't win.

Oh, when the children left the house, Tom acknowledged my challenges, but he never admitted that he did not do enough of the parenting. That might be the way it is in every family. If the mother stays home, she does most of the parenting. In a stepfamily, it is often harder for the stepmother or stepfather to parent the stepchild. So goes life. I have to look forward now.

It was time to leave the reception. The newlyweds were leaving and everyone was saying their goodbyes. I truly hope they have a wonderful life together and that they have the passionate love for each other that Tom and I do. That does not mean there are not going to be tough times — no one is perfect. We, Tom and I, have both had our struggles. But if you truly love each other and can keep those feelings alive so you remember them as the years go by, then chances are, things will be okay.

As I closed my eyes to fall asleep, I felt my husband's loving arms around me.

"Jo, I love you, and thank you for making... No, for allowing this day to be special. I know that it was hard for you. I understand. Good night."

Well, I guess it was all worth it!

Chapter Two

Tom

My wife always says I am a complicated man. I think I am very simple, really. I was raised an only child. My parents had me late in life. My mother, Anne, had several miscarriages before I was born in 1954, so they were thrilled, at their mature ages of 42 and 46, to have a child.

My mother always pushed me in regard to education. My earliest memories are of my mother reading to me or taking me to a museum. I guess she was too old to play games with me. I am not complaining at all — I never knew any differently. My life centered around education and church, and I read at an early age, and played the piano by ear. My father was always at work, and I remember that he came home with a smile on his face every day.

My mother and father sent me to kindergarten when I was four. Everyone was older than me, but since I was already reading, the teacher allowed me to read to the other students before we took a nap. I loved to organize games at recess, and my teacher said I was a born leader.

After two months of kindergarten, the teacher called my parents in for a conference, and said she thought it would be a good idea to move me into first grade. I had just turned five. They were shocked, and were not so sure this was a good idea. The teacher started to tell my mother stories of me in kindergarten, reading to the class, organizing games, etc. They all finally agreed it would be the right thing to do. So, they moved me to first grade.

I remember feeling a little awkward the first few weeks. I already knew how to read and count, so I blended in well. I seemed comfortable with the lessons, and I felt comfortable with the other children even though they were older than me.

This began my educational life. I surfaced at the top of every class and had a desire to be the best at everything I did, no matter what it was. I received good grades and was very competitive.

As I got older, I wanted to earn some money. I hated asking my father and mother for money. So I started to mow lawns for the neighbors and worked every weekend doing any odd job I could get. I found a new love — work!

I had a passion for starting something and seeing it to fruition, if you will. My mother often said to me, "It is a joy to watch you grow up." She was the loving force in our family. My father was loving too, but not demonstratively. I felt that unconditional love that every child needs to grow to be a healthy human being. I was very lucky to have the parents I did and will be forever grateful.

I figured out that, by working hard, I could have anything I wanted.

I loved the challenge and really did not understand that not everyone felt the way I did.

At age 12, I made so much money that I bought a new lawnmower in preparation for the next summer's work. It was a beautiful machine. It propelled itself and, all the years I used it, it never had a problem. I wish they were made that way today.

Work did not take up all of my life. I have to admit I had a mischievous side. My good friend Tony and I loved to ride our bikes into the woods. We would build forts and sleep in them overnight. We roamed the woods and neighborhoods many nights. Back then, things were so different. "Boys would be boys," and they were allowed to make mistakes. That was how we learned.

One night, when we were 14, Tony and I decided we wanted to learn how to drive a car. After our parents went to sleep, we quietly got in Tony's father's car, put it in neutral, and pushed it down the road.

Tony's father had a garage in town, and Tony worked there a lot. He was very familiar with cars. Tony said he knew how to start a car without the keys. Two blocks away, Tony jumped in the car and popped the clutch. It started, and we drove around town.

The first block we drove was not too bad. Tony was a good driver. It was a thrill, and I still remember that feeling today!

"Okay, now it's my turn," I said. "I know how to drive." I had NEVER driven a car!

Well, it was unforgettable. I made the front page of the local newspaper.

"Watch out!"

"Oh, God! What did I hit?"

I not only took out a stop sign as I was turning the corner, I also hit a neighbor's car and ran over a cat.

"Oh, no! We killed a cat."

"Is that all you are worried about? Look at the car!" Tony yelled. "My dad is going to kill me!"

"Let's bury the cat in the woods!" I said.

We put the cat in a garbage bag and buried it. To this day, the family thinks the cat just ran away.

"Oh, no. Look at the car!" The sun was coming up and I could see the damage so much better!

"This is not going to be fun," I told Tony. "I will be grounded forever."

My father made me go to Mr. Boyd's house and tell him what happened. I apologized and said I would pay for the damages.

My father paid him for the car repair, and I had to pay my father out of my lawn mowing money. I had to mow Mr. Boyd's yard for the next three years to pay off the damage. That hurt, but it was probably one of the most valuable lessons I learned in my childhood.

I continued to work in the summers and eventually paid off all my debt.

When I graduated from high school, I wanted to go to college. I saved my money and knew I could afford one year. Then I would have to work my way through the last three years to finish my schooling.

I enrolled at the local university. Business was my course of study. In one of my classes, I met a nice girl named Alice, and I asked her out on a date. We enjoyed our time together and continued dating that first year. Alice seemed to know me very well. She was attentive to my needs. Often she would meet me after one of my classes and have a donut and coffee for me. I think I was a challenge for her because, as I look back, I was not attentive to her needs. I was determined to get through school and start a career. If she showed up with a donut, that was great.

I never really dated in high school, because I was always too busy working. Oh, I went to the prom my junior and senior years, but that was about it for my social life in high school. I honestly do not know what drove me. Why did I work so hard? Was this characteristic innate? Did I just want the money? Was it what you were supposed to do back then? Who knows? I know working made me happy and I don't think anything could have changed me.

I also knew that if I wanted anything, I had to work for it.

Alice's father had a car dealership and needed some part-timers to help out on weekends. That is how my life really started. It paved the way for my future. I did not want to waste four years without making a paycheck, so I sold cars for Alice's father. As I said, I am naturally competitive and I soon became the top salesman at the dealership. I did all this while going to school and, because of my hard work, I did not have to take out any school loans. I did have to take a leave of absence from my junior year of college.

My father developed lung cancer, and Mother was having a hard time taking care of him. I went home one weekend and it broke my heart to see how hard she was working. I knew she could not continue on her own. She was taking care of him and fielding all the calls from his work. Dad was a cash register salesman, and he traveled a lot.

I knew I had to drop out of school and come home to help take care of my father. In those days, you didn't hire anyone to come in and help. Besides, we could not have afforded it, and health insurance did not cover anything like that. My father had no disability insurance, and I'm not sure there was such a thing back then.

I loved and respected my parents, so one day I went home and said, "Mom, I will quit school and work to help out." She cried. She would never have asked me to do that, but I knew I should.

I went to work full time for Alice's dad. He had come to depend on me in the dealership, and was glad to have me full time. Mom understood, and was thankful I was willing to help financially.

This situation changed my whole life. My father recovered from his illness after a year, and was able to go back to work. I went back to finish my business degree at the university.

Two years after I graduated, Alice's father was ready to retire and sold me his dealership. He knew I would be successful, and so did I. I did not even question it. When I was young, I just made a decision and did it. It was just the way it was.

And then it all started...

I asked Alice to marry me. She said yes. It was a lovely, but small and quiet wedding. Just a few of our closest friends and family attended. Within a year, we bought a small house. Life was perfect, or so I thought.

As I look back, I thought it was "scripted." I did not deviate from the norm.

Get a job, take care of your wife and family, and all will be well for the rest of your life. Was there anything else?

Did I love my wife? Not passionately, I am sure of that. But our relationship was convenient at the time. She was nice, and I won't lie. I wanted to buy her father's business, so getting married to Alice seemed like the right thing to do. We got along very well, like good friends.

Alice was working at a bank, and she definitely seemed to enjoy being married and "playing house." Alice wanted to do the things her friends were doing, and she followed their lead. After a year or so, several of her co-workers were pregnant.

She went to several baby showers, and it was becoming obvious to me that she wanted to have a child. I really didn't care one way or the other, and I thought she would be a good mother. Why wouldn't she? She loved playing house, and that was the next step. Children, right? The father brings home the paycheck and the mother raises the children and does the housework. I thought my life was perfect. It was the way I grew up.

Alice got pregnant and had our first child, Andrew. We were very happy for a while.

For the next few years, I had one focus. That was to support my family; food, clothes, shelter, education. As I look back, it was scary.

I went to work every day with a mission to do whatever it took to do just that. Pretty soon, our family grew to be four. We had a daughter, Sarah, three years after Andrew was born. She seemed so fragile, so tiny — I was overwhelmed with the thought of supporting my family. Sarah seemed so helpless. Why didn't Andrew seem helpless when he was born? There is a difference. At least there was for me. It seemed like Sarah needed to be taken care of. On the other hand, I had to teach Andrew how to take care of others.

Andrew and Sarah became the most important people in my life. As time went on, I was not so sure Alice was as devoted to the children as I was.

Alice seemed more concerned about getting her nails done and shopping than staying home with the children. I recognized this somewhat, but allowed her the luxury of getting babysitters and housekeepers. I indulged her every wish, even though I saw her slipping away from me and the children. Alice was changing.

As the business grew, I changed too. I realize that now. I felt a great sense of ownership and wanted to have the best car dealership in the area. I employed about 30 people. I loved my work and I think my employees loved working there.

I just ignored the changing situation between my wife and me. I know now that was wrong, but I continued to work hard and take care of my family. I thought our family struggle was just a bump in the road.

Alice was still the same. She was dependent on me for everything. Of course, she did not work anymore — she was raising the children. I expected her to be the devoted housewife and mother. I chose not to see what she wasn't doing at the house.

Andrew had just started school and Sarah was in preschool when I started to realize things were not working out between us. I soon realized what was not happening, and it was our relationship.

I worked all day and wanted to come home in the evenings to spend time with my wife and children. The kids were okay, but Alice was not happy.

One evening I walked in the door and asked, "Alice, what's for dinner?"

"Oh, Mr. Walden, Alice is out for the evening and she didn't tell me you would be home or I would have made something for you to eat."

"I am sorry, but who are you?"

"I am a friend of Alice's. She called and asked me to babysit this evening. She told me she would be home before you, so I did not think to make you dinner."

"Okay, what are the children having to eat? I will eat what they are eating, I don't need anything special."

"Well, they are having chicken nuggets and tater tots. I will heat some up for you."

As I grabbed a beer, Alice walked in the door. She was surprised to see me home. I didn't usually come home until 6:30 or later, and it was only 6:00 p.m.

Since I hired a nanny and a housekeeper to help Alice with the cleaning and children, I was thinking about asking Alice to help a little at the dealership.

I pleaded with her, "Alice, I could really use your help tomorrow. I will have two employees out. Would you please come in and work for the day? All you have to do is answer the phones. The children will be at school and, for the life of me, I don't know what you do all day."

"Tom, you know I have my schedule planned one week in advance. You have to give me more notice. I promised to help Sharon with the children's holiday party at school." After that, Alice walked away saying how tired she was.

"Alice, I need your help," I yelled, as she was walking up the steps.

No answer. I heard the bedroom door shut. "How hard can it be to buy candy for a child's party?" Again, no answer.

The next night I added up everything I was spending on household expenses, and decided that I could live alone with the children and continue to have the housekeeper and nanny. Not much would change for the children. Just Alice.

I could raise the children on my own. I did not need Alice. She actually cost me much more money than the children. Funny, the decision was made so easily, so matter-of-factly. I knew what I wanted to do, and once I made a decision, I accepted it. There was no emotional reaction from me.

Alice was never home anymore, anyway. She always had an excuse to leave town to visit her family or friends. She went without the children, which meant they had to have a babysitter much of the time.

So, one Sunday evening I asked Alice for a divorce, and the conversation was surprisingly simple.

"Alice, what are we going to do about our relationship?" This got no response from Alice.

"Alice, do we stay together or not? If we do, then you are going to have to start holding up your end around the house and with the children. I am not going to pay for a full-time nanny and housekeeper when you are not working."

To my surprise, she said, "Okay, let's get a divorce." We worked out the details of the divorce agreement, which were very simple. We both had a college education and both wanted to work, so we decided that when I had the children, I would pay for whatever they needed. When Alice had them, she would buy what they needed. No alimony sounded pretty good to me. We then set out on our individual ways. We just did not get along. Family and neighbors were shocked. No one had any idea there were any problems with our marriage.

The other thing was that back then, couples usually didn't get a divorce just because they didn't get along. Again, I did not care about what other people thought. I just wanted to take care of my children and my business.

Alice moved home to her parent's house. She didn't think she could take care of the children financially and she was not opposed to me raising the children, as long as I took care of all their financial needs. That was okay with me. The only sticking point in all of this was the one conversation that she never let me forget.

"Alice, I will take care of the children. You won't have to pay anything as long as they are living with me." She agreed. She never let me forget those words.

"I want to visit them and have some time with them on a regular basis, Tom." I had no problem with that.

"Anytime, Alice. I feel the children need us both in their lives." The divorce seemed to go too easily.

Shortly after we separated, Alice realized she needed, or wanted, more income than she was able to make on her own. She asked me to give her alimony on top of the divorce settlement and I said no. It wasn't for the kids, and she had an education. I felt she should support herself. Alice did not like my response at all, and I started to see her true colors at this point. She then sued me for alimony.

This was a terrible time in the children's lives and mine. I chose not to discuss our financial situation with the children. How could they possibly understand the financial matters of adults? I felt all they needed to know was that they were taken care of, and I would be the one to do that.

Alice, on the other hand, led them to believe that she was suing me because I did not want to take care of my family. They didn't understand the things she said, and worried about how this would affect them. They were scared. Would they be able to eat? Would they have clothes? There were some tears, and I had to sit them down and explain that I would always take care of them and they had nothing to worry about.

When they would ask why Mom was so upset, I would tell them, "That has nothing to do with you. It is between your mother and me. Don't worry about any of this — I love you and we will be just fine."

I said it with such passion. I wanted them to trust in me. I now realized that Alice would use them against me in any way she could to get alimony.

I couldn't figure out how to explain alimony to the children — there was no good way. They would just have to trust me.

I had a good attorney who was able to prove that I was fulfilling the roles of both the mother and father in our family situation, and the court decided in my favor.

What really bothered me was Alice's willingness to be dependent, and her desire to take money that wasn't owed her. She was young and healthy and could work again. It was evident she could take care of the kids, but she just didn't want to. She was perfectly capable of getting a job and supporting herself.

When we were married, she did not clean the house, wash the clothes, or take care of the kids. We hired someone to do everything. Hell, if she had made an effort to do what a housewife and mother normally would do, I would have given her the alimony she wanted. But I had to pay for all those services. Alice did not want to be in a partnership when we were married, and I was determined I was not going to be the one to support her when we were not.

I am a common sense kind of guy. I think I do what is right when it comes to most situations. I knew Alice would not starve, and it was time she grew up.

I realize that I sometimes use avoidance techniques to deal with challenging situations, and I should have gotten out of that marriage long before I did.

Chapter 3

After the Divorce

Alice did not work, nor had she made any effort to find a job. After she moved home to her parents', she rarely saw the children. Ironically, she actually had more formal education than I did, but she wasn't putting any of that education to use.

Alice graduated from college with a degree in business, and had done very well at the bank where she worked after we were married. But after the divorce, she never applied for a job. She did this thinking that she could persuade me to pay her living expenses.

For several years, Alice bad-mouthed me. She said terrible things to anyone who would listen, but I didn't have the time to pay any attention to the rumors.

Alice said things like, "Tom left me destitute. He would not even pay for the credit card charges we had accrued for the children. He left me with the old car, and I had to have repairs done just to make it safe! He lives in our house, and I have to live with my parents!"

People had no way of knowing that the credit card bills had nothing to do with the children. They were for her clothes, makeup, nail salons, etc. I paid her for her share of the house and the car. She had more than enough money to put a down payment on a house and buy a new car at the same time. I also gave her $50,000 cash, thinking it might take her a year to get a good job. I thought I was very generous.

The children started out visiting Alice on weekends, but that slowly decreased over time. She always had a reason why she could not see them, and it seemed like she just didn't want to be a parent. Oh, she liked having them, but didn't seem to want the responsibility that came along with them. There were always other commitments that were more important, and Alice could not squeeze in the kids during that time.

Eventually, Alice just said, "Tom when they want to see me, let me know.

I will come get them."

That was fine with me. I loved having them, and the weekends were better for me because I did not feel rushed because of work. I never tried to make Alice feel guilty about not seeing them. It was working for me.

Alice eventually got a job and moved out of her parents' house. She moved back to town to be closer to the children. She was a secretary for the local Catholic Church, which was a good job, and I hoped being around the church might be a good influence on her. She even started spending more time with the children, and not just on the weekends.

Alice would often tell me I was doing a good job raising them. I liked the changes I was seeing in Alice, and times like this reminded me why I married her in the first place. We were actually getting along better now than ever and, for a fleeting moment, I wondered if we should try to reconnect.

When I started dating Josie, all of this changed. It's funny how things change when a new person enters the picture. I really liked her. She was easy to get along with and I was hoping she would like the kids. Josie did not have any children and had never been married before. I told the children she was a friend.

After a month or so, Alice realized that the friend I was seeing was a girlfriend.

Frankly, I had no desire to talk to Alice about my personal life anymore, and I felt it was none of her business. The kids were happy, I was happy, work was going well. Life was good.

I started seeing some changes in Alice's demeanor when she came to pick up the kids. She started asking me questions like, "What are you doing tonight?" or "Do you have plans for this weekend?" She would claim she needed to know because of the children and her schedule.

That was strange, and she became even more curious. I just ignored her behavior and hoped it would go away, but it didn't. She continued to question the children about my "friend." Alice was definitely jealous that I was dating.

You know that old saying, "You always want what you can't have?" Well, that applied here.

Chapter 4

Josie

Tom and I met through his attorney. I worked in the law office where Tom got his divorce. I watched him come and go when he had appointments, and I knew he was interested in me — almost from the first time we met. We had a connection. Before we went on our first date, I thought about him every day at work. I just knew he was the one for me. Tom would come to his appointments earlier than necessary, and then he'd sit in the waiting room and talk with me.

It took him about six months to ask me out, and when he did finally ask me to dinner, I felt like we already had a relationship. His divorce had just been finalized, and I could tell he felt a lot of relief. We did not mention his divorce or ex-wife at all. The dinner was very casual, and very long. We spent a lot of that time just learning about each other.

We talked about our families, growing up, our hobbies, likes and dislikes, and we talked about how we both loved to work. We had a lot in common, and we could have talked all night. We had so much fun getting to know one another, and I was so focused on Tom that I don't even remember what I ate for dinner that night!

Finally, he said, "Josie, I guess we should go. We've been sitting here for a while, and I think they need our table for other customers."

As we walked to the car, Tom asked, "Do you think it is too early for you to meet my children?"

Although I was very interested in Tom, I was surprised by his question.

We hadn't even kissed yet — was it this serious already? I was very attracted to him, I knew that.

"Well Tom, I suppose it is okay. Just introduce me as a friend."

He stopped, looked at me, and then kissed me. At that moment, I knew we would be more than just friends. The attraction was undeniable. We didn't say a thing on the ride home. I was thinking about my future with him and what it would be like. I was not sure what he was thinking, but I was hoping it was the same.

Tom and I returned to his house to meet the children. He had hired the next door neighbor to babysit while we were out, but we were in for a surprise when we went into Tom's house.

"Alice, what are you doing here?" Tom asked.

Alice was on the living room floor playing with the children.

"Who is sick?" he asked

"No one," said Alice. "I stopped by to give Sarah a book and told the neighbor to go home when I saw the kids were here alone."

"They were not alone, Alice! I hired her to babysit!"

My instincts immediately kicked in, and I didn't say a word, but just stood there and listened.

"Alice, you can go. I will call you tomorrow, and we can talk then," Tom said, trying to get her out the door.

Alice questioned the arrangement, saying "How will you get her home? The kids probably don't want to ride along, and you know how we both feel about having them stay alone."

"Alice, you know I would never let them stay alone!"

Alice stared at me. I knew she recognized me, but she did not realize where she had met me. She had come to the law office several times to meet with the attorneys. I remembered her, but she could not quite place me.

Alice tried to stall, saying, "Sarah, Andrew, don't you want to finish our board game?"

Of course they did. That was a dirty trick!

I went out on a ledge and said, "Tom, why don't we take them for ice cream on the way home?"

He said, "Great idea!" Situation solved.

If only things were that easy for the next 20 years! Ice cream can fix a lot when they're little — that's for sure.

I think Tom liked the fact that I was able to figure out what was happening with Alice in such a short time frame. Alice didn't like it one bit.

That first date was indicative of what the rest of our life would be like.

Tom and I continued to date. We had a great relationship, and I spent time with his kids once or twice a month. We had dinner three or four times a week, and sometimes I met him at his house during the day to eat lunch.

That was my favorite time with Tom. He usually made lunch. We would share a sandwich and then share our love for each other. The passion we felt was real. I could not love anyone more. It felt great to love someone and know they loved you back, and I could tell that he did by how he looked at me. I had never experienced that before and, honestly, it was hard to be away from him. I thought about him every minute of the day.

As Tom and I began to see each other more, Alice began questioning the children about me. They could not satisfy their mother's curiosity, because all they knew was that I was a friend of Daddy's, and that I liked ice cream.

So, Alice started questioning Tom about me. Tom is a very private person, so that didn't go anywhere. He just avoided seeing and talking to her, and she definitely did not like that.

Early on in our dating, Tom always dropped off the kids to Alice before he picked me up, and the children didn't know he was spending the day with me. As time went on, I started to meet him at his house and ride along to take the kids to Alice's.

This annoyed Alice, and she became even more inquisitive about our relationship. If Tom was five minutes late, she would chastise him in front of me and the children. Really, I thought. What is up with this lady?

One day, as we pulled up the driveway to Alice's house, she was sitting on the front porch waiting for us.

"Josie, would you please take the kids inside while I talk to Tom for a minute? It's really important."

I agreed, although I was more than a little uncomfortable going into Alice's house. When I went inside, I noticed pictures of Tom and Alice on the wall, and more standing in frames on almost every piece of furniture that could hold something. What really shocked me was their wedding picture on the TV. She was living in a fantasy world. She definitely knew what she was doing when she asked me to walk in her house. She was staking her claim!

"Tom, have you ever been in her house?" I said, with a very concerned look on my face.

"Sure. Why?" Tom said, ever so innocently.

"Well, she has your wedding picture on the TV, and pictures of you two and the kids everywhere. I understand you were a family but — the wedding pictures — really? She is still living in that world."

"Yes, I know she's having a hard time separating from our past, Josie."

"Hard time? She needs help — seriously. She needs counseling, Tom."

"Well, that's not my problem anymore," Tom said. "If it starts to affect our relationship, I will talk to her, okay?" That was the first time Tom ever spoke to me in a matter-of-fact way, and I was not sure I liked it. Was this indicative of what was to come if we got married? Or did his ex-wife just upset him and he reacted?

That should have been my first clue as to what was coming. In retrospect, I think I knew, but I didn't want to believe that anything could hinder, hurt, or destroy our relationship. When you want something that badly, you're willing to justify why it is good for you.

I never mentioned it again. I was so profoundly affected by what I saw when I walked into her house, and I was hurt by the way Tom responded to me. Our relationship was too young to start an argument over his children, not that I would ever want to do that, but wow — he was touchy.

After that, I tried to make sure we met her at the perfect time — and that we were on a schedule so she could not get Tom's ear and upset him. He never told me what was so important that Alice had to talk to him alone that day. I knew she just wanted me to see the pictures of their family.

When future situations arose, Tom would tell Alice, "Call me. We should not discuss this in front of the children." Alice used the children a lot to get what she wanted. Tom did not like to argue with Alice at all, and used the avoidance technique when dealing with her.

Another thing Alice liked to do was to drop the kids off at Tom's after her weekend, when she had a friend with her. Of course, she always walked them into Tom's house, saying things like, "Oh, this was my painting, but Tom kept it," or "I picked out this sofa, and painted the room. Tom, this room needs repainting."

The worst part was that when she first came into the house, she would yell "Tom, the kids are home. I have Sally with me. Come say hello to an old friend."

Tom would stop doing whatever he was involved in and say hello. He wanted to be polite. Alice would occasionally recognize me if she could not avoid it. She would say, "Oh, hi Josie," and then walk away. It was always the same comment. Tom was always neutral about these situations, but Alice was encouraged because she had his attention.

Alice was all smiles while she led her friends around Tom's house.

"It has been awhile since you have seen Susan. Tom, doesn't she look terrific?" she would say, leaning into Tom and touching his arm.

I would think, does he not get what she is doing? Honestly, has he never had a psychology/sociology/human behavioral course?

She was owning a time in his life, and making sure I knew I was not part of it, by having a conversation with Tom that I could not join. I guess that made Alice feel important.

These conversations would go on and on, until something would interrupt him. "Dad, the phone is for you," or "Dad, I'm hungry. What's for dinner?" He never knew how to get out of those conversations with Alice, and didn't realize the things Alice was doing to drag him into them in the first place.

"Should we meet here or at my place, Tom? What is better for you?"

Sometimes, she would ask Tom to pick up the children at her friend's house, where she would try to create a social atmosphere between her, Tom, and the kids.

She'd say, "Hey Tom, play a little basketball with us before you have to take off." She knew I was sitting in the car.

I had to point this one out to Tom and fortunately, he was a quick learner.

Alice started to come around Tom's house unannounced, and Tom felt this was okay, because he thought she wanted to see the children.

I knew better. She wanted to see if I was there, so she could figure out exactly how much time I was spending there. She would walk into Tom's kitchen, help herself to coffee, and even put dishes away, saying she knew right where they went.

I asked Tom if he felt this was appropriate now that the house and things inside it belonged solely to him.

"Oh, I don't care, Jo. She just wants to spend time with the kids."

"But Tom, when she does that, she is not spending time with the kids.

They're in their rooms and she is pretending to be your wife again, putting away the dishes, and folding the kids' clothes. Don't you see that her behavior, and the fact that you're allowing it, is awkward and inappropriate?"

"Jo, I don't look at this emotionally, I suppose you're right. If it makes you uncomfortable, I will ask her to stop coming in after she drops them off."

"Yes, it does make me uncomfortable," I said. He did not have a clue as to what Alice was up to, and since I had no formal connection to Tom at that point, I didn't really feel I could tell him what to do. Besides, I have to admit I was curious about how far he would let this go.

Women seem to be more emotionally driven than men, and Tom didn't attach emotions or ulterior motives to the things Alice was doing. I thought Alice knew exactly what she was doing, and she was hoping Tom would see her in a good light and come back to her. I'm not sure that was what Alice really wanted — she just didn't like to play second fiddle. I don't think she really wanted Tom; she just didn't want me to have him.

The more I saw Tom, the more she showed up, and this really started to bother me. I wasn't sure I could handle all this baggage, but I was quickly falling in love with Tom. I thought his love could help me handle anything that was thrown in our path.

I think the thing that bothered me the most was that we didn't have much time to be together intimately. One or two days a week, we tried to take long lunch hours and meet at his house. The kids were in school, and Alice was at work. I loved those afternoons.

We needed that time together, with no interruptions from the kids, no business, and no Alice! It always felt right being with Tom. I was very inexperienced with sex, not that I hadn't had it, and I was definitely not confident about my skills. He was kind and gentle with me, and it was always so hard to go back to the office. I never stopped to consider how we would fit our personal time in if we were married.

Then, the unbelievable happened! One day, Tom and I were home at lunch and Alice pulled up in the driveway. Uh-oh! We felt like we had been caught, and I later wondered why we reacted like that. We both got out of bed and started to get dressed. We didn't hurry; we never thought she would come into the bedroom. We were two adults in love, and we just wanted to be together.

Tom forgot that Alice still had a key to the house. As I expected, she walked in and started yelling, "Tom, are you here? Is one of the kids sick?"

And then there she came, right into Tom's bedroom. I was half dressed, and Tom was only a little more decent than I was.

"Alice! What are you doing in here? Please leave now!"

She left the room, went to the kitchen, and helped herself to a cup of coffee!

Tom walked into the kitchen, where Alice greeted him by saying, "This coffee is too strong. Don't you use Folgers anymore?"

Oh. My. God.

"Alice, what are you doing here?" Tom asked, ignoring the coffee.

"I saw your car," she said, not mentioning my car in the driveway. "I thought one of the kids might be sick."

"Everything is fine, Alice. I am busy. I will talk to you when I drop the kids off on Friday."

"Tom, why do you have Josie here?" she said very quietly.

"That is none of your business, Alice. What are you doing driving by my house?"

"It is my business Tom, especially if you do this when the children are around." She ignored his second question. I had a feeling she drove by the house a lot.

Somehow we managed to get through that next 20 minutes. I walked downstairs and stared at her with a serious and firm look on my face, but I did not say a word.

Tom spoke for both of us, saying, "Alice, you need to call before you come to this house again."

Alice walked out the door, and Tom and I went back to work. Things were not so easy after that. Alice definitely felt threatened, and she always had some reason to come inside the house when dropping off the children.

She never walked into our house at lunchtime again, and Tom didn't ask her for her key back. I never did understand that one.

One afternoon, Tom told me he could take the whole afternoon off, and asked if it would be possible for me to get the afternoon off also.

"Sure," I said. "Are we going somewhere?"

"No," Tom said. "I just want a little more time alone with you."

We met at noon. When I walked in the house, Tom had a dozen red roses on the kitchen table.

"They are beautiful!" I said.

He took me in his arms and kissed me. "I love you Josie, and I want to spend the rest of my life with you. Will you marry me?"

"Yes, of course Tom. I love you." Nothing else needed to be said that afternoon. Tom led me to his bed and we slowly caressed each other and made love for the next hour.

Tom presented me with a beautiful diamond ring. "Amazing," I said. "It is lovely, and you didn't need to do this. I would have married you without it." Tom put it on my finger, and it fit perfectly.

I could see Tom was deep in thought. "Tom, what are you thinking about?"

He finally touched my face and said, "I know I need to get the situation with my ex-wife under control. I promise I will do that."

Up until that moment, Tom and I had never mentioned his ex-wife's name in our bed. That was an unspoken rule, and one we both understood. That was the one and only time, and she was never again mentioned in our bedroom.

It had been a year since Tom and I first started dating, and getting engaged changed things for me. I started to feel a sense of ownership for our lives.

Every time Alice came to the house now, it bothered me. Tom and I decided not to move in together because of the kids, but I was at Tom's house a lot.

As time went on, Alice started pushing the limits again.

One day I got to Tom's house after work and found Alice in the kitchen making sandwiches for Andrew and Sarah.

"Oh, they get hungry after school," she said.

That night, I decided to approach Tom.

"Tom, I stopped at the house today and Alice was there. She sent the babysitter home and was making sandwiches for the children."

He called Alice that moment. She was not home, so he left a message.

"Alice, this is Tom. I hire a babysitter for the children after school for two hours every day. If you would like to pick them up at school and take them to your house, please let me know. I will reduce the babysitter's hours.

Please do not show up at the house uninvited."

Alice never responded to the phone message, and Tom never followed up.

Never mind the fact that she was now overstepping her bounds and coming into what was no longer her home uninvited! Her goal was to monitor my relationship with Tom, and I didn't like that at all.

Another incident occurred just a week after Tom left the message for Alice. This time, it was a Saturday morning. The children were still in bed, and God knows how Alice found out that Tom was at the dealership. She was probably stalking him.

I had told Tom I would relieve the babysitter and bring the children to the dealership, and then we would all have lunch. When I walked in the house that morning, the kids were in bed, the babysitter was gone, and Alice was in the cupboards.

"Alice, I do not appreciate you coming to the house uninvited. It is inappropriate, and we have discussed this with you. Please leave."

"Oh yes, I remember — that afternoon." She was talking about that afternoon when she came to the house and into Tom's bedroom, of course.

"No, Alice. I mean when Tom called and left you a message last week."

I was not prepared for this interaction, so I called Tom and told him what was happening. As I was on the phone explaining the situation to Tom, Alice said, "Oh, all right. I'm leaving. I just wanted some time with the kids."

I said, "Alice, just call and we will bring them to you any time!" My face was red and I was so furious that I'm still surprised I was able to compose myself enough to say anything decent.

Not too long after that, I sat down with Tom and had a discussion one evening when the kids were at their mother's. He could have either ME or HER in his life. I refused to come home and see his ex-wife at the sink, helping herself to coffee or making sandwiches for the children!

There had to be some rules. He agreed. He also apologized and said he would try to consider things from my point of view.

The first thing he did was change the locks on the house. This helped immensely.

The next thing we did was to decide on a date for our wedding. We were both in agreement that we would get married as soon as possible. Andrew was nine years old and Sarah was six. The children seemed happy about our engagement, although nothing seemed real to them yet.

We discussed going away to get married. We had already planned a short vacation around one of Tom's business meetings, and we thought we'd just slip away, get married, then return and celebrate with the children. It seemed like a pretty good plan.

I discussed this with Abby, a good friend of mine, and the closest thing I had to a sister or confidant. She really became my therapist. I depended on her more than she will ever know. She always made such good sense, and I always tried to listen and evaluate everything she said to me. Abby and I were best friends growing up. We walked to school every day, did our homework together after school, and often ate at each other's homes. We were close, and she just always seemed to know what was best. We had not talked much over the past few years, but when we got together, there was an enduring bond. I have always trusted her judgment and still do today.

Abby warned me that eloping would be the worst thing we could do.

"The children have to be part of the wedding if they are going to accept your marriage. They have to feel special, too."

We discussed this at great length, and she was afraid the kids would be bitter about not being invited to their father's wedding, and that anger could manifest itself in different ways in the future.

Tom and I talked about Abby's recommendations. It was very complicated, this step environment. Tom finally said, "Jo, I agree with Abby. I absolutely feel it can't hurt. Why not involve them if it helps them to accept the idea of their father getting married?"

"Great, let's discuss it with them tonight. But Tom, if we tell them the date, we just might have an unwanted guest." I was very apprehensive about letting Alice know our wedding date.

"You're right," Tom agreed. "Let's not tell them the date, but let's have them prepare for the event. That way we can get all the details completed and tell them at the last minute. That is a very good idea!"

"Jo, combining the business trip with our wedding may not be such a good idea. The business trip is next month. What do you think? Is that too soon? Can we make all the arrangements?"

"Well, we are involving the children now, so we can have the immediate family over to participate in the ceremony and then go on the business trip. That might work. Let's make it a surprise for everyone!"

"We can plan it as a weekend get together. It will be Valentine's Day."

The trip was centered on an auto manufacturing convention, and we had decided to go early to see some of the sights before Tom attended the convention the last few days of the trip. It seemed to be a perfect solution to our situation.

Abby said she would help me with the wedding details, so we planned the wedding for Saturday, February 17th. The kids had school the next week and Tom's mom and dad had already said they would watch them.

Tom took Andrew to rent a tux, and I took Sarah to find her perfect dress. She was thrilled! Sarah said she wanted the dress to be "bridesey."

"I want it to flow on the floor, Jo. I also want it to be white, like your dress," she said.

"Well, I suppose that would be okay. Let's not focus on white, just on finding your favorite dress. What if your favorite dress is pink?"

"Yes, I want my favorite dress, even if it is pink, or blue, or red, or purple, or...."

"I get the picture, Sarah." We both laughed, and off we went to the only bridal store in town.

"Jo, what kind of shoes can I wear with it? How about high heels?"

"Well, that would be your father's decision. Let's find the dress first and then look for shoes. If they happen to have heels, we will call your father and ask for permission. What do you say about that?"

"Yeah, I am sure they will have heels, Jo. You can't wear a bridesey dress without heels. That would look really stupid!"

Sarah ended up with a white dress with pink trim. It really was beautiful, and I was so glad I told her white was okay. Sarah was allowed to wear small heels and stockings, and she felt very grown up.

As far as Sarah was concerned, this would be the best wedding ever. Her dress and shoes outweighed the fact that her father was getting married to his girlfriend. At her age, a new dress and shoes could work wonders!

Boy, I had a lot of lessons to learn about raising kids. I got lucky on that one.

Sarah was watching me as I tried on dresses. She daydreamed about the wedding, and she definitely had opinions on which dress I should wear.

With every comment and smile, I felt a little closer to Sarah.

I picked a white satin dress. It was short — not the traditional wedding dress — but I loved it, and felt good in it. Sarah approved of the dress, and we were ready to get married.

The time flew by and, all of a sudden, it was February 14th, our wedding day.

We called our families earlier in the week to invite them for a special Valentine dinner. Little did they know that when they arrived, they were attending a wedding. Tom's mom and dad knew the day before, and we told the children that morning. Boy, were they excited!

We definitely waited until the last minute to tell the kids. To this day, I am still not sure how we pulled that off. They didn't have time to think or analyze what was happening. Good or bad, that's just the way it was.

The children were so busy that week with school and the thought of relatives coming to stay for the weekend, I don't think it ever occurred to them that we might be having a wedding so soon.

My brother, James, who is in the Air Force, made arrangements to come to the wedding. Both of our parents were deceased by then, so it was just James and a few cousins from my side of the family, and my dear friend Abby, of course.

I was a nervous wreck that week. I was helping the kids with their homework, then trying to arrange catering for a nice sit-down dinner at our house for 30 people. Somehow, it all worked out.

Abby was still a little concerned that we were leaving the children behind, but there was just no way we were taking them on our honeymoon. That was too much to ask! She felt we should go away with them first, and then take a honeymoon later.

Neither Tom nor I agreed with Abby's suggestion regarding the honeymoon. Little did I know that we should have taken her advice. But, you can't rewrite the past, just learn from it.

Everything you can do as parents to ease a change, especially a change as big as having a new mother in the house, is worth it. Oh, well. There's no point looking back. What's done is done!

The children woke up that morning as if it was any normal day. Tom called a family meeting and told the kids that in four hours, we would be married. Sarah asked if this was the day she got to wear her new dress and shoes.

Andrew was quiet. Tom was quick to notice that he had to involve him.

"Andrew, would you please work with the DJ and suggest songs that he should play for the guests?"

"Wow, Dad! Yes, I will." He was excited.

Everyone enjoyed themselves at our wedding, and they all seemed happy for us. Sarah, in her little heels, beamed all day long. The children felt really special. It was a great way to start our new family life. I was also glad we decided not to leave until a few days after the wedding. This gave us a chance to enjoy the day with Sarah and Andrew.

It really was a great day for all of us! Well, excluding Alice, of course.

Not that she was at the wedding. She found out about it the next day.

Evidently one of Andrew's friends told his mom, who called Alice. It had to happen.

A mutual friend of ours told us that Alice felt she should have been involved in the wedding. Alice said she needed to be there to "ease the pain" of her children watching their father get married to someone else.

Yes, Sarah did have pain. Her feet hurt from walking around in those shoes all day! Andrew looked like a young man in his suit. Everyone told him how handsome he was, and he was smiling all day. He felt very important.

Alice had gotten wind of our wedding plans earlier from the children, though she had no idea when or where the wedding would take place. Tom and I both agreed that it would be best not to tell her until after it was over.

When Alice asked Tom about it, he just shrugged and said, "We will let you know if we need your help with the children or anything."

It was easy to see that Alice felt threatened and insecure. She no longer had Tom as her husband, and I think she saw us as a happy couple. I believe she turned green with envy.

So Tom and I were married, and the kids and our families seemed to enjoy the day. For some reason, the children did not talk about or comment on their mother that day. I think they knew that this life would be separate from her and they did not have to report everything to her that went on. I sensed this, but did not understand any of it.

Chapter Five

The Early Years of Our Marriage

The newspaper said, "Thomas Walden and Josie Regal were married on February 17, 1990. They exchanged vows along with Thomas' children, Andrew, 9, and Sarah, 6, by their sides."

I was 31 years old and married for the first time in my life. Tom was 36, and this was his second marriage. We were so in love, and I felt so blessed to find my soulmate. I never thought I would find someone that I cared for so passionately. Just having him beside me made my heart jump.

As I read the newspaper, I told Tom, "The picture is beautiful." I said this, knowing our life would be a fairytale. How could anything go wrong? He was a good father, and I knew he would be a good husband. How could I ask for more?

"Tom, I know we will be fine forever as a married couple. I know that because of the feelings and passion I have for you." I needed to open my heart and let Tom know how committed I was to our relationship.

"Josie, the first time I was married, I married because it was the thing to do. I felt obligated in a way, because I worked for Alice's father. He was so good to me. Alice and I dated and, after we graduated, getting married was the next step. This time, I married for love. It can't get any better. I love you."

I knew Tom loved me. I could feel it. It was such a good feeling to know the person I was with loved me completely. I had heard about this type of relationship, but I had never experienced it before Tom. A lot of my friends got married and were not really sure if they had that passionate love for their husband. But they had been together as couples for a long time, and they felt it was time to get married and start a family, whether they were in love or not.

Practicality set in quickly. We couldn't just get married and go off on a honeymoon. We had to make sure the children were taken care of.

We waited a few days to go on our honeymoon because Tom's parents had some medical appointments that could not be changed. They stayed with the children while we were away. We also wanted to make sure they were fine before we left. I now had several brand new dimensions in my life that I had to consider before making plans of any kind.

Children were a big change for me. I had always done what I wanted on the spur of the moment. I never had to check on a dog, let alone a child or arrange babysitters.

In a way, Abby got her wish. We spent our wedding night with the children, and it was good. We spent half the next day talking with Andrew and Sarah about the wedding day events. We had breakfast when the kids woke up, and they immediately started in.

"Andrew, did you see me dancing with Uncle James?"

"Yes, Sarah I did. And did you see me breakdancing? Everyone was watching me!"

"Josie, when will the pictures be here? I can't wait to see my dress."

"Sarah," Andrew said. "Didn't you look in the mirror?"

We all laughed and laughed. This was family fun, and I could not wait for the rest of my life to continue.

Tom's parents were very dear. They were very supportive of our marriage. Since Tom was their only child, I expected them to be more possessive of his time. Instead, they had made him very independent. Good parents!

They lived very close by and were willing to help whenever necessary. Tom had needed their help the past few years, raising the children on his own.

His ex-wife had been seeing Andrew and Sarah one weekend a month, and Tom was very flexible when it came to her visits. He wanted her to be involved. He always tried to accommodate her when she asked to see the kids. He knew this would be beneficial to them in the future.

Tom did not feel it would be appropriate to ask Alice to keep the kids while we were on our honeymoon. It just felt awkward to him, I guess. I was not sure about this decision, but could not and would not give an opinion at that point.

I was so excited to get away alone with Tom to celebrate our new life together. I knew this probably wouldn't happen again for a while.

"Tom, I'm all packed, and so eager to spend a few days alone with you. I love your children, but it will be nice to be alone with you."

"I know, Jo. I feel the same way. Andrew and Sarah will be taken care of." And then he said, "The phone is ringing. Don't answer it! It could be Alice. We are not going to talk to her today."

Tom put his arms around me and kissed me passionately. We could not keep our hands off each other. The children walked in and just giggled.

Tom ran after Sarah, saying, "Get back here, you little stinker. I'm going to tickle you!" Of course, Tom caught Sarah, and Andrew even got in on the action. The laughter was contagious. I thought, what a beautiful life we are going to have.

"Jo, the cab is here. Time to go!" The kids ran to give their father a hug.

I smiled and waved goodbye. The children were not quite comfortable showing their affection to me yet. They were very respectful and smiled and told me to have fun. I hoped they would someday run to give me a hug also. I yearned for that family bond.

I wanted to enjoy each moment of my honeymoon, and was prepared to have the greatest week of my life. Canada was just a few short hours away. We boarded the plane, hand in hand.

All the passengers had to know we were newlyweds, but we didn't care. We were so happy! Canada was the one place I had always wanted to visit.

Tom knew that, and when he suggested to me that we make Canada our honeymoon destination, I was elated.

We were on our way to a beautiful bed and breakfast in Montreal. We could not stop looking at each other. At that moment in time, we were all there was. Nothing else mattered.

Our first night was bliss; we held each other all night long. I wondered, could life be this perfect? We surfaced from our room at noon the next day, ready to enjoy some of the sights.

We spent the first afternoon window shopping. There were so many things to see and do. I don't think I really saw what was in the store windows. We were so in love. We couldn't stop holding hands; we had to be touching constantly. I just kept thinking about our life together and how wonderful it was going to be.

It was beautiful that time of year in Montreal. The snow made everything picture perfect. It was very, very cold in the evening, and all the more reason to snuggle a little closer. About 8:00 p.m., after a wonderful dinner, we returned to our room. I went into the bathroom to put on my nightgown and, little did I know, our honeymoon was about to come to an abrupt end.

I heard the phone ring, and Tom said, "Honey, I'll get it."

Then I heard, "What? Where is Sarah now? In the emergency room! What? Oh, my!" Tom said in a worried voice.

I wasn't too worried. I figured Tom's parents would know what to do with any situation and, after all, this was our honeymoon. Wouldn't Tom's ex-wife be available for emergencies?

When I came back into the room, Tom said. "We have a problem, and you may want to sit down."

That did not sound good.

"I'm so sorry, but we have to go home now," Tom said as gently as he could.

I was stunned. "What happened?" I said, concerned.

"Sarah broke her leg in gym class. She is in the emergency room having it set as we speak," Tom answered.

"How could you decide this without speaking to me first, Tom? Can't your parents take care of this, and where is Alice?"

"Alice cannot be reached, and I do not want to burden my parents." At that point, Tom stood up and started to pack. I could tell there was no other option. I had a feeling Tom had not tried to contact Alice, and I was really upset.

"Okay," I said. "I guess we have to leave." Emotionally, I was not fully on board with this decision, but I could see that Tom had made up his mind.

As I was re-packing all the new clothes that I had bought for this trip, I realized how selfish I was being, and I felt awful. I should have shown him more support. It just caught me off guard, and I responded before I had time to consider our role as parents, rather than newlyweds.

It is a scary thing for a little girl to break her leg. I guess we had no other choice.

"Okay, you're right. We should go," I said, voicing my support.

It was not easy getting a flight home. We sat in the airport for several long hours before we were able to get on a plane. Tom was so worried that he hardly heard a word I said to him. He just sat and looked out the windows.

Tom admitted that he didn't even try to call Alice, and I felt this was wrong. I tried to tell him that she had a right to know, and that I would be furious if my child was in the hospital and no one notified me.

Tom's response was short and to the point. "I'm not calling Alice!"

When we arrived at the hometown airport, it was 2:30a.m. We picked up our luggage and went straight to the hospital. Tom's mom, Anne, was sitting in the emergency room. Tom stayed with Sarah and I went home with Anne, where her husband, Tom Sr., my new father-in-law, was staying with Andrew.

I definitely did not understand everything that was happening, but I realized that over the years Tom had pretty much taken on both parenting roles for his kids. Where would I fit into this picture?

When I walked in the house, Andrew was sleeping downstairs on the couch.

He looked like a little angel. I leaned over and kissed his cheek. He woke up, ever so gently, and started crying. I am not sure if it was over Sarah, or just that he was homesick for his father, and maybe me. He crawled into my arms, and I was smitten. This little boy and I would become best friends. Tom was right; we needed to come home. Maybe in Andrew's mind this was a test. He seemed so relieved to see us.

"Boy, are we glad you two are home," Anne said. "We are exhausted." They looked it! When I told them to go to bed and get some rest, I barely got the words out before they headed for the stairs.

Andrew was worried about his sister, and just as we started to talk about Sarah's broken leg, Tom came through the door carrying her.

She had a cast on her foot and leg, and the hospital staff had already autographed it in different colors.

Tom said, "It's a clean break, and they were able to set it. She has to have the cast on for 12 weeks. They said it will heal quickly."

"Thank heavens it wasn't any worse." I replied.

We spent the rest of the night and until noon the next day catching up on our sleep, all of us together on the family room floor with Sarah's leg propped up on several pillows. It was a good night.

I felt as if I had my own family. Maybe this was why Tom rushed home so quickly. I had a lot to learn about raising a family. It was at this point that I decided to make them my own.

Step Changes I should have made:
1. Counseling for myself.
2. Help with parenting skills.

Chapter 6

Creating My Own Environment

Alice came over that day to check on Sarah. I tried to understand that she was Sarah's mother, and of course she would be concerned. I even offered her a cup of coffee. She was hell-bent on seeing Tom, and I also understood that. They were Sarah's parents, and Tom had been the one who talked to the doctors and brought Sarah home from the hospital.

But the first thing Alice said to Tom was that he should have told her about his wedding plans. She said she would have counseled the children so they would not be upset.

Did she ask about Sarah? NO! She just continued to chastise Tom for not telling her about the wedding.

Tom raised his voice and said, "The kids are happy, Alice. We have a good relationship. If you want to take Sarah with you for a while, please feel free to do so, but she has homework to do and she has to stay up with her schoolwork while she is absent."

Alice started to cry, said something to Sarah, and ran out of the house. We did not hear what she said, and we did not ask Sarah. We both thought it was interesting that Sarah did not want to go with her mom, and was not upset when Alice left. That whole scenario indicated to me that Sarah was comfortable where she was — with her father and me.

I think the worst part for Alice was that she saw us as a happy, functioning stepfamily. This was going to be more complicated than I thought. Besides having to learn the parenting thing, I would have to learn to deal with an ex-wife.

Alice tried all sorts of deceptive tricks to disrupt our family balance.

If one of the children did not do their homework, she would call the teacher and tell them that I let them stay up too late.

She would visit mutual friends of ours and try to alienate them from me by telling them, "Josie does not know how to be a mother. The kids are constantly calling me to come and get them."

Of course, they were all lies. Well, maybe not all of them. I was not sure how to be a mother. I had a good role model in my own mother, but my mother never had to deal with the dynamics of a stepfamily. I tried to do what I thought my mother would have done in each situation that arose.

Normally, that would have been a good philosophy, but step-parenting involved so much more energy, emotion and money than I anticipated.

Alice became obsessed with our relationship. She continued to pour fuel on any fire she could find or create! I realized that Tom and Alice's friends would not become our friends. Tom could not comprehend this. Maybe the men would continue to be friends with Tom, but the women? No way.

Alice had them convinced that I was evil, immature and a husband stealer! I tried to be around them, but it got harder and harder as time went on. I had to convince Tom that we needed to develop a new social circle.

I decided that the best thing to do was to focus on Tom and the children and stop worrying about Alice. I started to throw myself into our family routine. I wanted to do the best I could raising Andrew and Sarah.

Every morning I was up at the crack of dawn. I had breakfast prepared, the table was set, and I waited for the children to come down. I wanted everything to be perfect, and I tried to be proactive. If there was a glitch, we could handle it.

In the beginning, everyone made an effort. Tom offered to help with breakfast, and the kids got up when they were called. It was hard to believe that children could be so obedient. I kept waiting for it to change and, now that I look back, I would characterize our daily routine as walking on eggshells.

Tom wasn't sure if I would be able to handle the stress of raising children. He never said it, but it was implied in his daily questions. Was I all right, were the kids obeying me, was I tired in the evenings? I was still employed full time, and it was stressful, but I was not going to let him know that. I wanted the three of them to think I could handle everything. Wrong, wrong, wrong. I should have asked for help.

Funny, it wasn't a burden when we were not married. I would work all day and then go to Tom's, pick up the kids and we would go for dinner. Many times, I cooked dinner at his house. That DEFINITELY changed after we were married. I tried hard to help Tom as much as I could. I think I volunteered to do too much. Now that I was married and raising Tom's children, my day job had become a burden.

I truly enjoyed my work as a legal secretary. It was a place where I could get away from the hustle at home. I felt appreciated at work, and I wasn't ready to give it up at that point. But, my job was eight hours of every day. How was I going to do it all?

My interactions with Andrew and Sarah changed slowly. The kids were not quite sure how to interact with or respond to me. The atmosphere in our house became a little more difficult as time went on.

If I asked them to do a chore, they said "yes," but much more slowly than in the first few months of our marriage. As time went on, their true feelings came out, or changed, for some reason.

I noticed the change in Andrew first. His behavior became passive-aggressive. He was 10 now, and I'm sure he had opinions of his dad's relationship with me, but he did not know where to place them on the spectrum of family. I am sure Alice was helping him make the decision as to where I should be on that spectrum.

Sarah was seven, and she was independent, naïve, and so innocent. She had no idea why her mother asked her so many questions about me. She would come home from Alice's and say, "Josie, what were you and Dad doing yesterday? My mom wanted to know." Or, "Does Daddy kiss you a lot? Mommy doesn't think so, but I told her he did."

Eventually, both children began to get feisty with me. I guess they were trying to get used to yet another authority in their lives. I am not sure I would have known how to deal with all the changes if I was in their shoes. I'm sure Alice was telling them that I was NOT their mother. In their minds, that meant they didn't have to listen to me, tell me about what happened at school, etc.

I talked to Tom about it. "It will take time, Josie. Be patient." I was hoping for a little more insight than that.

The children were not disobedient at school. They listened to their teachers and did their homework. I constantly reminded myself that, at school, they did not have the emotional factor of sharing their father with someone else.

Now Andrew and Sarah had a new person sitting at the table, joining in all their conversations, giving orders, and participating in their everyday activities. It had to be hard, especially with their biological mother, who was not present, telling them their new stepmother was not a good person.

"That is not your cup!" Andrew spouted one day, as I took a sip of my coffee.

"It is now," Tom said sternly, giving Andrew a pointed look.

I was standing there, not knowing what to do, and Tom came over and held my chair for me to sit down. He said, "Please sit down and enjoy your coffee."

After breakfast, as I walked Tom to his car, I said, "What happened in there?"

"Well, that was their mother's coffee cup. It is going to take them a while to get comfortable with you in this house. Maybe we should consider buying a new house."

"I agree, Tom. This house feels like it has a ghost. I'll start looking immediately — maybe one with a pool?"

"Good idea," Tom said. We both knew that, with both our salaries, we could probably afford it.

When I got home from work that day I threw out that coffee cup!

I continually tried to treat the children with the utmost respect. I never disciplined them. Their father was the only one who grounded them or took things away as a punishment, etc. I always asked them to do their chores in a kind voice. But if they did not do them, I did not force them. I just told their father when he got home from work. I knew that was not good because then it looked like I was telling on them and, in retrospect, I was. I didn't think I had any other options.

Simple things caused major problems. I was brought up to be polite and mannerly. Using please, thank you, and God bless you when you sneezed, was commonplace in our house.

In Tom's house, I seldom heard these words. I guess he was too busy to think of everything and, from what Tom has told me about Alice, she was not into the teaching aspect of being a parent.

One day, Sarah said to me, "I want some ice cream." I said to Sarah, "I want some ice cream, please." She said, "Yes." Well that was a start. When I handed her the cone, I said, "What do you say?"

Andrew replied, "She doesn't have to say anything to you. You are not her mom!"

Wow. Where did that come from? Andrew was harboring big time feelings of resentment. He certainly did not want me to parent him. That was obvious.

Sarah was still standing there. Before I handed her the ice cream cone, I put a little extra scoop on it. She smiled and ran off, yelling, "Thank you."

Well, I was halfway there, one kid down, one to go. When I gave Andrew his ice cream cone, he took it quickly and ran outside. So much for please and thank you.

Things only continued to get worse with Andrew. He responded to me with sarcasm in everything he said.

If I said, "Andrew, it is time to get up for school."

He said, "I'll get up when I'm ready."

If I said, "It is time to go to bed," he said, "You are not my mom, and you can't tell me what to do." Everything became a power struggle. He usually won. I was losing the battle very quickly and I had no idea what to do besides report my interactions to Tom.

I tried talking to Tom about Andrew's attitude. He did not want to hear it.

He was tired every day from work. When he walked in the door, he just wanted to relax.

"Tom, I am tired too, but you need to get a handle on Andrew before this blows up. How about if you tell him what he is supposed to do each night, maybe a note or something. I will not remind him, and then he will not have to respond to me. He will have to answer to you."

That worked for one week. Then Tom slipped back into asking me to relay messages to Andrew.

The problem was that Tom did not want to handle discipline. He had so much stress at work. He insisted I handle things as they come up, and not wait for him to get home.

Tom didn't understand that, when HE asked the children to put their bikes away, for example, it was an insignificant, unemotional, generic request.

If I asked them, it was a much bigger deal.

Sometimes the bikes were outside for four days, rain or shine. I was determined not to put them in the garage. It was not my job! When Tom came home and saw the bikes out, he directed his remarks to me, rather than the kids.

"Didn't you ask Andrew to put his bike away?"

"Yes Tom, I did. He didn't listen to me. Maybe you should have a talk with him."

"Did you ask him nicely? What was your tone?"

"Yes, I asked him nicely!" I said with frustration.

Tom continued to say that the reason Andrew did not listen to me was because of the tone of my voice when asking him. So, the next day I tried again.

"Andrew, please put your bike in the garage, it is raining and it will rust."

"I will."

"Please do it right now," I said. "It is raining hard."

I remember that my mother always said, "You never ask a child to do something without saying when they have to do it." If you don't give them a time, they will do it when and if they get the urge, which might be never.

Andrew responded "You are not my mother!" and he ran out of the house.

It was a power play, and definitely a big emotional deal in their eyes! How could I ask them to do such a thing?

Tom could not get his head around this concept. He just thought things could be said and done in a simple way.

I tried, but the kids did not view my requests, no matter how generic, in a simple way! I refused to punish the children; it was not my place. I knew if I tried to send them to their rooms, they would not go. So, I just told their father when he got home. That created lots of arguments between Tom and me.

The next day, Tom was home early, and the kids did not realize he was home.

Andrew walked in the door, threw his book bag on the kitchen table as hard as he could, then looked at me.

I said, "Andrew, please don't throw your book bag on the table. You're going to break the table. Please take your book bag to your room now."

"You are not my mother, and I do not have to listen to you!"

Just then, we heard, "You do have to listen to what she says. Now take that book bag upstairs immediately." Then, Tom walked away.

I did not understand why Tom left the room after his comment. He could have at least acknowledged my struggles or asked Andrew to apologize.

At least he saw how Andrew was responding to me when he was not home.

Before that moment, the children did not know how their father would respond to them when they did not obey me. They became cautious with their responses. If Tom was around, they responded quickly, but if he was at work, Andrew's rude response was typical.

I realized that as soon as Tom let his guard down, things began to happen.

One morning, I was very disappointed when Andrew and Sarah did not have time to eat. They slept as late as they could and just had time to throw their clothes on and run out the door to catch the bus.

Tom always left early for work, and I was left to deal with the situation.

I worked at 9 a.m., so I had time to get the children off to school. If they missed the bus, I drove them. Big mistake!

It was a Thursday, and they both had busy weeks at school, tests, lots of sports practices, meetings, etc. Truly, there were times when I did not know how the children kept up with everything they had to do.

Anyway, I shouted one more time, "I am leaving now. You have missed the bus. I will have to take you, and I do not want to be late for work. Please hurry up."

No response.

Sarah came down dressed and ready, "May I have something to eat? He will not be ready for a while."

Now, I was angry! I handed Sarah a banana and marched upstairs.

"Andrew, what are you doing?"

"I'll be there. Just a few more minutes." He said it so casually, it made me fume.

"Not in a few minutes. You are on my schedule now and I won't be able to get to work on time."

"I'm coming," he said, moving slowly.

The kids were late to school. I was late to work. Sarah was still hungry.

When Tom got home that evening, Andrew was quick to run downstairs and give him the note from the attendance lady, which explained that when children are late to school, parents/guardians must walk them in to school and fill out a slip, stating the reason for their tardiness.

Another argument ensued between Tom and me. We went to our bedroom to discuss it, but Tom's voice traveled all over the house when he got angry with me. His question was always the same.

"How did you say it?"

"Say what?" I answered, not believing that he was questioning ME.

"How did you tell him? I think it is the way you say things that makes him not respond to you."

At that point, Andrew stormed into our room. He had heard everything, of course. I had repeatedly asked Tom to lower his voice, but he just got angrier and talked louder. He saw no reason not to let the children hear our arguments.

That ideology really bothered me. When I grew up, it was important for parents to have their discussions/arguments privately. My parents believed that a child could not properly assess adult discussions. What was Tom thinking?

"She yelled at me, and I started to cry, then I had to go to the bathroom," Andrew complained, as his tears began to flow. "It's is all her fault!"

"Tom, I am going to talk to you in a calm voice. I am doing the best I can. Andrew won't listen to me. I think it is time we see a counselor, before we lose all love and respect in this family."

"No, I won't see a counselor," Tom said. "I will handle this."

Children in newly formed stepfamilies have all the normal stresses of the school day and then, on top of that, they have the added emotional stress of trying to figure out where they fit in their environment.

It wasn't Tom's children's fault. They were too young to understand all that was going on, and it seemed like they felt pushed aside in a world where they used to know the dynamics. They had to figure it out with no help from their father, and it wasn't fair to them or me.

Counseling would have been beneficial for our stepfamily. That was our biggest mistake!

On top of all that, we had to get the kids to eat in the morning. How could they learn at school if they were too hungry to concentrate?

"Tom, you will have to get them breakfast before they go to school."

"Go ahead, Josie — call them 15 minutes earlier. It would be good if they ate something in the morning before school."

I wanted him to handle it. I guess he had other thoughts, and our lack of communication was creating a huge problem.

The next day, I woke them up 15 minutes early, then woke them up again and again. Finally, they walked down the stairs at their normal time. It was not working. I was not able to get them moving in the morning.

This became a major battle, and nothing I tried seemed to work. They were basically refusing to do anything I asked.

Our situation continued to deteriorate, and I was the only one trying to make it work. Our family structure was breaking down.

Tom finally agreed that we both had to be involved, and that he needed to take on the majority of the load. That was great in theory, but didn't really work since I was the one at home with the children most of the time.

Arguments between Tom and I happened over and over again, and I was fed up!

One evening I told Tom, "My schedule has changed, and I have to leave for work every morning at 7:45. You'll have to stay home until the kids get on the bus."

Tom got up, looked at me, and stormed out of the room. He did not speak to me for three days. He had a decision to make, since I was not taking them anymore. Would he drive them to school or make them take the bus like the other neighbor kids? At that point, I didn't care. They were his children, and he could handle it.

I was at a low point, and I realized it should not have taken me that long to come to that decision. I was also tempted to leave him. Did he not see the problem here? He should be responsible for his own children. They could not understand why their dad had relinquished all the childrearing to his new wife. The children were certainly not listening to me.

That night we were all sitting at the dinner table. I thought I had prepared a nice meal. We had macaroni and cheese, meat loaf, and peas. I knew the kids liked this meal, but the attitudes showed up quickly.

"This isn't as good as Mom's," Andrew said. "I hate peas!" He started stirring the food around on his plate.

Sarah looked at Andrew and said, "I am not even hungry." She started to cry. She put her head down on the table and would not look up. I looked at Tom, and he just shrugged his shoulders.

I got up from the table and walked out the door. I had had it! There was a coffee shop within walking distance, and I went there and had a cup of coffee. I had no intention of going home until the kids were in bed. A neighbor from across the street saw me and came up to say hello. I tried to be polite, but I think he could tell I was stressed. He asked if everything was okay, and I assured him that it was. We made small talk for a couple of minutes and then he left, thank heavens.

After two cups of coffee and a lot of thought, I started the walk home. Tom never came to look for me. Then it occurred to me. How could he? He had two children to take care of. He couldn't leave the house.

I was raised to be happy and positive, and I had never been in that type of environment. I went from living a life that was happy, with a family who loved and respected me, to feeling disrespected and hated.

I really tried to be understanding. Tom had been working hard. He had a lot of stress, and shifting the childcare to me alleviated some of it. I knew it wasn't right, but as a woman, I could not stop myself. Working became my only respite.

I did not want to monitor the homework, send them to bed, or wake them up in the morning. But when each situation arose, I handled it. Why couldn't I just get dressed and go to work, like Tom did? I waited to see if Tom would handle things first, but he acted like he didn't see what was going on.

I tried to blame it on Mother Nature, and told myself that men just didn't see what women see when dealing with children. I really needed some counseling. I needed to know HOW to handle my step situation before I went crazy trying to figure it out!

My mother always told me, "If you can't put your children to bed when they are young, you will have a lifetime of problems." I related this to not being able to get them to school on time. Was I going to have a lifetime of struggle with them?

Our family dynamics were terrible, and no one was happy. Responses from Andrew were always sarcastic, and discussions with Tom were even worse.

It occurred to me that Alice was behind a lot of this discord. She was no doubt probing the kids with questions and planting situations in their mind.

Alice tried her hardest to be a part of our family. She continued to show up at our house at unexpected times, and she called constantly to talk to the kids.

It seemed as though Alice was interfering even when she was not at our house. There was no distance from her, and the kids seemed bothered by her constant badgering. Having their mother question them about their home life and their father's relationship with his wife was not normal! Alice had become obsessed with our daily routines.

She was continuously forcing herself into our lives. She showed up at our house one evening when we were entertaining couples from my office. Sarah and Andrew were in the car, and they were supposed to spend the evening with her. Alice came back to the house with the excuse that Andrew wanted to play a certain board game and she did not have it at home. Instead of sending Andrew in to get the game, Alice came in and introduced herself as "Tom's first wife."

Our guests had heard her name before because they had handled the divorce, but they didn't know much about her personality. They were learning fast.

Alice smiled and walked around the room, chatting, apparently forgetting why she had come.

I just stood there, getting madder by the second. Tom saw that I was embarrassed, and reacted quickly.

"Alice, I need to talk to you about the kids. Let's walk outside," Tom said.

Alice agreed and, as she was walking past my boss, said, "He always wants to talk to me about the kids. I don't think his young wife is very experienced." She said it just loud enough for me to hear.

Tom practically pulled Alice outside and said, "Alice, you are being disrespectful to Josie. Please do not come in our house uninvited anymore. You were very inappropriate in there."

"Boy, you are not friendly anymore, Tom. I need to go back in and get my purse."

"Here it is, Alice," I said as I walked out the door. I handed her the purse and turned to Tom.

"Come on, honey. Our guests are waiting for us." We walked back in the house, arm in arm. I would have given anything to see the look on her face.

She left without the game, which was just an excuse to get in the house to see who we were entertaining. Alice was definitely in denial.

I wondered what she would have thought if I had shown up at a party of hers and said, "I am Tom's new wife. He divorced Alice. She did not know how to be a mother to his children."

Tom and I worked hard the first few years. We truly wanted the children to feel loved and taken care of. I sacrificed a lot, and I became frustrated at times when the children would not listen to me.

By that time, I only had five more years until Andrew left home and went to college. I thought I could handle it. The problem was that I was the only one trying. I should have gone to counseling, even if I had to go alone.

My bitterness towards Alice and my frustration with the kids manifested in denying Tom sex. I was so emotionally exhausted that when he came to bed, I just turned away from him. He knew, but he was too tired to care or take the time to work things out.

I had let it go too far, and now I just felt used. The children were not seeing the love in our eyes anymore. It was very sad, and what was happening in our household was exactly what Alice had hoped. Everyone was mad at each other. We were all falling apart.

The children had no idea they were supposed to try, and all our conversations became strained. They had no one to talk to who could be objective, and their mother was making the situation worse. I was becoming less and less patient with them. Tom was like a robot, going through the motions and pretending that nothing was happening.

Andrew seldom, if ever, listened without an argument, and Sarah occasionally pretended she did not hear me. I think some of that was natural for their ages. Sarah was never hateful in her response, and I truly did not feel my relationship with Sarah was compromised. Sarah was younger and did not have the anger that Andrew did over the divorce. His mother talked more to him about what was going on with her and his father.

But life went on. There were bills to pay, homework to be done, and there was always the ex-wife. She was a mother who did not want to raise her own children, yet still wanted her ex-husband to take care of her. She inserted herself into our lives, and I was at the breaking point.

One day I turned to Tom and said, "Great, let her cook the meals, tutor the children, and make them do their chores! I don't care anymore. I can't do it all myself."

He just stormed out of the room.

And then one Friday afternoon, it happened. I lost total control of my mouth.

I walked into our house after work and saw Alice, with Andrew and Sarah, going through a box of pictures from our chest. The babysitter was gone, and we had no idea Alice was coming.

I asked her to please leave, and I tried to say it nicely in front of the children, but I am sure it sounded stressed.

She responded, "Oh, I will only be 15 or 20 more minutes, Josie."

"No, Alice. Please leave now. You can finish this with the kids this weekend."

"Okay, just a minute," replied Alice.

When that minute turned into 10, I called Tom on the phone and told him we had an emergency. Alice and the kids overheard me telling Tom he had to come home and get Alice out of my house.

"Josie, you are upsetting the children. I just wanted to spend an hour or so with them. You have them most of the time and I miss them." Alice said, putting her arms around both of them as if I was going to snatch them up and take them away. Her actions spoke even louder than her words. She was telling the kids they should not like me.

"Alice you are more than welcome to take them to your house or out for the day. You know Tom encourages that," I said, trying to get the situation under control.

"Oh Josie, this house was mine and theirs, and I want to keep things as normal for them as possible," Alice said.

I looked at the kids and said, "Andrew and Sarah, this is between your mother, your father and me. Please go upstairs and let your mom and I talk alone."

"You are crazy, Josie, and I don't know why Tom married you. You do not know how to raise children. My family was never like this when I was married to Tom."

She still had her arms around the kids, so of course they weren't going to listen to me and go upstairs.

And wow, that was so inappropriate to say in front of the children. The damage from her words would take me years to repair. It was evident she was trying to destroy any sense of relationship I had with Andrew and Sarah. Her words validated their feelings, and they would probably feel justified in their negative responses toward me. I had no idea how I would I ever regain a sense of respect in this family.

Alice was being a selfish, spoiled brat. How could anyone destroy the emotional wellbeing of their own children? She should have been encouraging the children to get along with me, and working with them to adjust to the changes in their lives. Alice did not have their best interests at heart, because it was always all about her. She was selfish, and put herself before her own children.

"Put the box of pictures down. If you want anything from this house, you have to check with Tom first. He is on his way home."

Alice continued to thumb through our wedding pictures, and I lost all control.

"That picture is mine! Put it back or I will call the police!"

Alice dropped the box. I guess she knew I was serious. But I had lost the battle. I had embarrassed the children's mother in front of them and, no matter what she had done, I could not do that. Ironically, she could yell at me, and they would not be fazed, but the opposite could not happen.

Tom came home a few minutes later, and Alice met him in my kitchen.

"I just wanted a few old pictures Tom. They were mine, anyway," Alice told Tom. "She did not have to accuse me of stealing." The children chimed in and told their father that I called their mother a "thief" and tried to kick her out of the house.

That drama did not end for several weeks. Our friends heard Alice's version, as did the teachers at school. I occasionally tried to tell my version, but in the end I just said, "Alice is not telling you the truth." People would eventually figure it out. My problem was that I feared the kids, who had no insight into these matters, would never figure it out.

I had to disconnect myself from the children. They were my husband's children, not mine. There was no way they were going to give me a chance, especially when their mother was blaming everything and anything on me.

No matter how hard I tried or how much I told myself that things could be different, it was irreparable at that moment.

The children knew their mother was not telling the truth about things that happened, but they were unable to admit it. The children had unconditional loyalty to their mother and they wanted her not to be sad anymore. They would support her no matter what.

One night shortly thereafter, I was not feeling well and went to bed early. At about 10, I heard crying and went downstairs. It was Alice, and Tom was comforting her.

She was saying, "Oh Tom, I should never have divorced you. I still love you, and I want my children to have a normal family environment."

I was livid. The children had to have heard her. What would they think? I could not believe what I was hearing! I walked into the kitchen, Tom looked at me with sad eyes. He felt sorry for her.

I walked away, and he later reminded me that he had a history with her and couldn't just forget about her feelings.

"Yes, you can! She is using you! She did not appreciate you when you were married. She was never home, and she didn't want to take care of her own children! Don't you remember any of that? She is emotionally abusing you and the kids! Tom, she says things in front of the children that are unspeakable. They have no way of processing what she says. They take everything at face value. If Alice says that I am an awful person, the kids will believe her. It has gone too far. She does not know how to have a decent, civil conversation. Alice is destroying our family!"

"Jo, I think you are overreacting. Of course I remember what she was like when I was married to her. That is why I divorced her. It is taking her a long time to accept all this. I know I should be taking your feelings into account, Jo, but you are not a parent."

I really should have walked out after he said that. What did he think I had been doing these last few years? I was stunned, and had no idea how to react. Tom did not have a clue.

In that moment, I became emotionally unattached to Tom. I was having second thoughts about whether I should have married him and, to compound things, I had also missed my period that month and feared that I was pregnant. I talked myself into believing it was stress. Tom and I had not discussed having a baby yet.

That night, I don't think I slept a wink. I tossed and turned, knowing instinctively that I was pregnant, but denying it. I wanted out of this marriage. I was done.

The next day I called Abby and said I needed to talk, and that things were bad. Would she like to go away for a few days? Thank heavens she said yes.

I didn't want to have a conversation with Tom right then, because I was afraid I would tell him about the pregnancy. So, I packed my suitcase and waited by the door. When Tom walked in, I stood up and told him my plans.

"Tom, this is all a lot for me to handle. I called Abby and we are going to the mountains for a few days. I have already taken off work for the next week."

"Really, you're going away with Abby." I could tell he was mad. His reaction bothered me. He definitely did not see this coming. He did not apologize for his part in the fact that I felt this way, or even sense that we needed to communicate our feelings regarding recent events.

I had never seen this side of him, and I could not handle this situation anymore. Tom refused to seek counseling, so I had to remove myself from the situation to be able to think clearly. I was so wrapped up in everything that I could not breathe. Everyone's problem became mine, and it seemed like I was to blame for everyone's problem in some way or another.

The first night I was away, Abby and I talked into the wee hours of the morning. She just listened and, when I was all talked out, she gave me some advice.

She said, "Jo, my friend, stay here for a week or so. Let him know what he is missing — not just the housework and care of the children — but your companionship. He has taken you for granted."

"I know you both love each other," she continued as I cried, "but every parent gets caught up in the day-to-day routines and activities. Biological parents have arguments like this."

That was an interesting way to put it. "Biological" parents. I wish Abby could have counseled Tom. She always puts things into perspective.

I thought a lot about what she said. When children are born, you grow slowly into their lives and learn what is needed from you as a mother or father at each stage. But when you are given children at an older age, you have not had those learning years as a parent to develop into what comes next.

Not only did I not develop into a mother from the early years on, I was NOT their mother. This was going to be tougher than I thought.

I thought about all of this a lot. Could I be what the children needed and wanted? I didn't know. I knew I could not do it on my own.

I was napping when the phone rang. It was Tom, calling to apologize. He missed me and wanted me to come home. I could tell it was hard for him to make that call.

Tom had learned to depend on me for a lot. I had literally taken a load of responsibility off his shoulders, including the cooking, washing, driving the kids to and from activities, and I was working full time. Now he was back to doing all of that himself.

Abby was standing in front of me, gesturing not to give in. I listened.

"I am sorry but I cannot come home now, I will see you in 10 days." I did not give him more than those few words, and I even extended my stay. I felt sick to my stomach. I wanted to give in and go home, but deep down I knew Abby was right.

When I lived alone, all I had to handle was me. I had taken on more than I should have in this marriage. I realized that Tom should still be handling the majority of the responsibility.

Meanwhile, back at home…

Alice walked into the house, and the children were doing their homework.

"Hi, Mom!" Andrew jumped up to give her a hug. "Josie left, she went to visit a friend and Dad said he does not know how long she will be gone. Do you want to help me with my math?"

"Sarah, did your father tell you this also?" asked Alice. "That Josie was gone?"

"Yeah, I think so."

Alice got right to work making chicken and sautéed veggies, which were Tom's favorite. She had the table set with linens. She did the laundry, which was piling up, and picked things up around the house. Then she sat down with the kids and waited until Tom got home from work.

Tom's Side

I walked in from a long, hard day, frustrated that I had the house to pick up and laundry to do. I sure wished Josie was home.

"Alice, what are you doing here?"

"Tom you need some help. Please let me do this. They are my children too, and things are falling apart around here. I made your favorite dinner, and the kids are hungry."

I was too tired to argue, so I let Alice do what she wanted and I went to bed. I did not want to start an argument with Alice. She was trying to help me, or so I thought.

The next morning when I got up, Alice was in the kitchen making breakfast. The kids were happy and they were already dressed. Unbelievable. Why don't the kids do this for Jo? I didn't even think about asking her where she spent the night. I didn't want to know.

When I came home from work I found the same scenario all over again, except this time Alice had wine and two glasses on the counter.

"Alice, what is this?"

"Tom tell me what happened. I can help."

I did not respond at first. I had a glass of wine and let my guard down, and I told Alice about the argument with the Josie. We drank the whole bottle of wine and I did not seem to care about the situation that was unfolding.

Alice put her hand on my arm and said, "Tom, I love you. I have always loved you. Give me a second chance. I know I made mistakes, but it will be different this time." She leaned over and kissed me.

I don't know why, but I didn't pull away. I felt a little guilty about what was happening, but thought about how Josie had left me and must not want to be married anymore, so why not? At that moment, Sarah ran into the kitchen when her mother and I embraced.

"Sarah, I am just comforting your mother." I could not think of anything else to say.

"Alice, I think it is time for you to go. I have to put the kids to bed."

"I can help, Tom." At that moment Andrew walked in.

"Yeah, Dad. Let Mom stay. Please?"

"Okay, just tonight." I knew she should not stay.

Alice helped put the kids to bed. She read a book to Sarah, kissed Andrew goodnight and even picked up Andrew's room.

Unbelievable, again! She never did this when we were married. Could it work again? Was Josie going to leave me? I needed someone to help out here. I was so confused. I worked hard every day to provide everything the kids needed, and I tried to be a good husband to Jo. Why did she leave?

What was I doing wrong? Was it the kids? Was it me?

Maybe Josie didn't know how to be a mom, and maybe Alice was right. But then again, Alice was not a great example of motherhood. And what was she up to, anyway?

Alice was there again in the morning, making coffee and getting the kids ready for school. They seemed happy and did not even seem to miss Jo.

I left for work and told Alice to lock up the house.

When I got home that night, Andrew told me that Josie called after I had left.

"Well, Andrew, what did she say or want?"

Andrew said, "I don't know, Dad. Mom said that when she answered the phone, Josie asked for you. That's about all I know."

Alice did not show up at the house the next night until very late, after I had the kids in bed. She called and said she was on her way with a surprise. She had a bottle of champagne and some salmon pate, and I loved every bite. It was a far cry from what I had been eating, which lately had been tater tots and chicken nuggets.

We drank the bottle of champagne, and Alice flirted with me. This time, I did not put up any resistance.

"Alice, Andrew said Josie called this morning and you answered the phone. What did she say?"

"She just said she would talk to you later, Tom. I think she was glad I was helping out."

The kids were in bed, and it seemed natural being with Alice. We did have two kids together. I have to admit, I was enjoying all the attention at first, then I started to feel a little uncomfortable. Alice started to belittle Josie, and I did not like that and started to get defensive.

"Tom, she is not a good mother. The kids have been upset and they do not like Josie. They say she does not help them with their homework and she makes them work like slaves with chores around the house."

"Alice, who is telling you that? I don't believe you. They are having a few adjustment problems getting used to another authority in their life. You could help, you know, by telling them they should listen to Jo and respect her. Frankly, I think you are alienating them from her."

I started to back away from Alice. She realized what she had done, and she started to cry, begging me to forgive her and give our marriage another chance.

"Alice, the only marriage I have is with Jo. I am going to work on that one. Now, please leave. It is time for you to go. You took advantage of my situation, and that's my fault. I promise it won't happen again."

Alice started to cry louder, and I was concerned about the kids waking up. I did not want them to witness this situation. They had already witnessed enough. Alice was so dramatic! The memories of my marriage with Alice were quickly coming back to me.

I went to bed and thought all night about how I was going to get Jo back. Alice must have called me 10 times the next day, and I ignored every call. I locked myself in my office at work and told my secretary not to let anyone disturb me.

Alice showed up at work, but she was not able to get past the secretary. About 3:00, I looked out my office window and saw Alice sitting in her car, watching the business. Was she stalking me?

I realized then that Jo was right. Alice needed help. I got up, walked outside to her car and said, "Leave now, please." And she did.

Jo's Side

"Abby, I just called home and Alice answered the phone. I asked what she was doing there and she said she was taking care of her children."

"What did you say to that? I thought you were not going to speak to Tom."

"I asked her to have Tom call me. And yes, I did say I was not going to call, but I was having a weak moment, I guess. I won't call again, that's for sure."

Abby continued to have good advice.

"Jo, you have a life also. You totally forgot you have feelings and needs as a wife and mother. You are even jeopardizing your work. Has Tom ever asked how you are doing, and if there is any way he can help you? Sometimes men are not very sensitive to a woman's needs, and his children are probably foremost in his mind."

She said this while standing two feet from me, looking directly into my eyes. I started to cry and told her I was pregnant.

"Oh, my," Abby said. "What are you going to do?" I realized that she intentionally did not give me her opinion on this one, but waited for my answer. Smart woman!

"I don't know. Right now, I want a divorce and an abortion."

I could hardly believe I said those words. I was also glad that I did not give in to Tom and return home. I could not think straight at that moment. My leaving would not have impacted him if I had accepted his apology without a conversation or understanding of the matter. Being away from Tom somehow gave me strength. I was more objective.

Abby just stared at me.

I said, "Please help me. I need to see a doctor to find out how far along I am."

The next day, Abby found a doctor who would see me immediately. She went with me, and sure enough, I was almost three months pregnant. I was so busy and caught up in all this "step craziness" that I did not realize that I had missed two periods. I had to make a decision quickly.

I spent the next two days crying, laughing, getting angry, and showing emotions — raw emotions I never knew I had.

Finally, Abby commented on the pregnancy. "Jo, this is not just your decision. Tom should be a part of this decision also. It is his child too." I knew she was right.

"As much as I would like to help you, you must go home and talk to Tom."

Then she turned to me and said, "What do you want from Tom? What do you want out of your marriage? What do you want out of life?"

I knew what I wanted. I wanted Tom's love and the children's love. I wanted Alice OUT of our lives. Most of all, I wanted this baby, because it was Tom's. But realistically, I did not know if I could have what I wanted.

Thinking about things at home just made me more upset. I was like a square peg in a round hole. Home was not working! I was not accepted there. It was not my house, because it had been Tom and Alice's house. Even the coffee cup was Alice's!

Abby and I talked and talked, and it was cathartic. Everyone should have a friend like Abby. She helped me organize my approach with Tom.

Not only did I have the situation with Tom and his ex-wife, but I had the challenging situation of the children. If I decided to stay married to Tom, it was not going to be easy.

Tom called one other time. He seemed to be desperate for me to return.

I had not made my decision yet, and I could not field another phone call from him begging me to return. I told Tom I would call him when I was ready to talk, then I turned off my phone.

Abby and I went shopping, hiking, and spent a lot of time talking. Tom was either going to know that I was serious about getting his support with the children, or I would ask him for a divorce. We worked through my questions around the relationship, and my concerns for the future.

If I had the abortion, would I regret it? Would I regret losing Tom?

I cared for Andrew and Sarah, and they would be out of the house soon enough. Would I have to wait to have a normal family? At that time, I did not believe that a stepfamily could be normal. A normal family laughed together, worked together, and loved each other. That was my dream family. I didn't think I could ever have that.

I wondered what the children thought about this new family environment. They must hate it, or me. They probably wished their mother was still living with them. We all needed help.

The children had been telling me with their actions that they were unhappy and needed some direction, but I didn't see it. That is because I needed some guidance in this crazy step situation myself. If I couldn't figure it out, why in the world was I expecting those poor kids to figure it out?

Abby and I laid out all kinds of guidelines that I could use in a discussion with Tom.

"Josie, the most important thing is for Tom to acknowledge that you were thrown into a situation that is almost impossible to come out of unscathed. Otherwise, he will continue to think that you can correct it alone. You can't!" Abby said. "Jo, he has to realize that he is the father and ex-husband, and he has to control the situation with both Alice and his children. You do not have an ex-wife or children."

Easier said than done!

I knew Abby was right. Tom expected me to be able to handle it all. Two children, a full time job, ex-wife, and a house. I could not handle it without his help. And I was not getting that help where I needed it most, which was with the kids and Alice. If the house or the job fell apart, we could handle that. But, all of us being unhappy every day not a good environment for any of us.

I called Tom two days before I was to return home. I wanted to meet with him before I returned to the house. That way I could talk to him in private regarding my plans for dealing with Alice and the kids.

"I don't think that is necessary, Jo!" Tom said. "Just come home. We will be fine."

"We won't Tom, and I don't think I could handle walking into the house and seeing Alice at the cupboards again."

"Josie! I love you."

"I believe you Tom, but the kids do not love me and I see them more than you. It is a stressful situation for all of us. You have the best of both worlds.

Someone to cook, clean, and parent the kids, of which I am not doing a very good job, I fear. I feel you are taking advantage of me."

Then I said, "I am not coming home if you don't do this for me. It is your decision. Call me tomorrow and let me know if you will agree."

The next day Tom called and said he would do anything I wanted; he just wanted me back. We arranged a place and time to meet. I had a lot to think about before I met him.

Tom took off work on Friday and met me at Starbucks. We sat in a corner and cried before we even started to discuss the situation. Neither of us could talk.

Tom listened intently to what I had to say. He agreed with most of it.

He also knew it was going to be hard to limit Alice's freedom with the children and our house. He said he was willing to try.

I suggested counseling, once again, and his response was, "No way!" He would never give in to that. That was the item I had to give up if I wanted to stay married to Tom. Before I left Abby's, I had gone to the bookstore and bought several books to take to our meeting. There were not many books on how to parent stepchildren, but I found a few with some references that related to our situation.

My next comment was startling to Tom. "I am pregnant — almost three months. I was so busy taking care of everything at home, I didn't even realize that I had missed two periods."

He didn't say anything right away, but I could see him thinking and was not sure what he was going to say next.

"Jo, I do love children and I will love our child."

"I am thinking about a divorce, Tom. I cannot live the life I am living. I am a slave to your children. They are disrespectful and, at times, bully me. Your ex-wife stalks us, and it is just more than I can handle. I will not live like this. Things must change or I want a divorce."

Tom started to cry. "I know I have put everything on your shoulders, and I am sorry. What can I do to make things easier?" This was all I wanted to hear.

We talked for a while longer and agreed on a plan to make our lives better. I showed him the books and asked if we could read and discuss them. I wanted to be educated on how to parent my stepchildren. Tom agreed.

After we talked, Tom called Alice and asked her to meet him at the park. She eagerly agreed, and I'm sure she thought this was her chance to get Tom back. She knew I had left, and she knew Tom was angry, but she did not know I had returned.

What she also didn't know was that I was joining her and Tom at the park. Boy, was she surprised when she saw me!

She was dressed to the hilt, in full makeup and heels. I thought, who in their right mind dresses like that to sit on a park bench and have a discussion? I knew when I saw Alice walk up that her mission was to destroy our marriage. She was shocked to see me.

"Oh. Hello, Josie. I didn't know you would be here." I just smiled.

"Alice, Jo and I have some things we want to discuss with you. Let me preface this conversation with the fact that we are doing this for the children. We do not want them to be stressed anymore. We are the adults and we need to guide them through this change."

"What change, Tom? They still have the same mother and father."

"Of course they do, but there is one more important person in their life now, and they are being disrespectful to her. It is not their fault. The adults are to blame. We have not set a good example of how to handle changes."

Tom included us in the blame, and that was good. He did not attack her with comments that made her defensive. It was a good way to start the dialog.

"Alice, I think we both want the children to have comfortable environments. We want the best for them."

"Tom, forgive me, but you are the one who got remarried. The children know they have all my love."

"The children know they have my unconditional love too, Alice. But they could also have a good relationship with Jo. And Alice, you may want to get remarried someday, too. How would you want the children to respond to your new husband?"

At this point I felt I needed to say something. I could see that Alice was afraid of losing the children's love.

"Alice, I don't want to be their mother. They love you and Tom very much and no one will ever take your place. I just want to be a friend to them and be treated with respect. Nothing more. When you ask them to make their bed, do they do it?"

"Yes, of course."

"Well, how would you feel if every time you asked them to do a chore, their response was, I don't have to listen to you."

It took her a while to respond. I think she was wondering what to say. She was probably very happy they responded to me with this tone, yet as a mother, she probably would not want them to respond to other adults that way.

Alice took the high road, even though she probably did not want to.

"Okay, I understand. What do you want me to do?"

We discussed our plan and rules with her. She listened. She shed a few tears, but Tom did not waiver.

"It is hard to have another woman in your children's lives," Alice said, barely able to get the words out.

We promised Alice we would not try to alienate her from her children, and made sure she understood we expected the same in return.

Just as Tom promised, we showed a united front to Alice. He put his arm around me as we talked with her, and kept his distance from her. His physical demeanor was perfect. I was so proud of him for supporting me.

Maybe this was what our family needed all along. The kids needed to see that their mom was okay with their dad's marriage.

The signal the children had been getting from Alice was that she was hurt badly by their father getting remarried, and that she was the victim in the situation.

The signal they were getting from Tom was one of total confusion and a refusal to choose a side.

Tom felt badly for Alice and didn't want to offend or hurt her, and he truly wanted Alice to be in her children's life, but she was causing distress in our stepfamily.

He loved me, but did not know how to fit me into his life and keep everyone else happy.

He wanted the children to have a normal life.

At the end of our discussion with Alice we gave her a list of conditions regarding her behavior and how it would impact the children's response to me. The list was thorough and very respectful:

- *Each parent will call and get permission before coming to the other's house.*
- *Please adhere to the designated schedule of specific days and times.*
- *Do not come inside the house unless you are invited by an adult.*
- *The children will be ready to go; call to confirm on your way to pick them up.*
- *Wait in the car until they come out.*
- *These rules are not to be shared with the children.*
- *Do not alienate the children from the other parent/stepparent.*
- *If there is a problem, the biological parents will discuss it without the children around.*

Alice grudgingly agreed to comply with our rules. She finally realized that Tom had made his choice, and he had chosen me.

"I understand and agree with you, but you should have told me you were getting married," Alice said. "It looked to the children like you were hiding that from me and that made them think there was something that needed to be hidden. It made things worse for them."

Tom validated her statement.

"Alice, it won't happen again. We all have to work together to make sure the children have a happy and emotionally healthy life. We both know the children will benefit from us making decisions and sticking to them. Then there is no emotional confusion."

At the end of our discussion, Tom looked at me and asked, "Is there anything you want to say Jo?"

I said, "No, I think that about covers it."

I should have thanked Alice for agreeing to accept the rules, but I didn't. I was like a kid getting my way, and I now had the power. I walked away with a grin on my face. It was definitely a satisfying moment for me.

I later realized how Alice must have felt and why she kept trying to control the situation. It made her feel as if she was in control of her children and her life, and it made her feel like she was winning.

As we got in the car to go home, Alice walked by us without saying a word. Tom called out to her, "Alice, thank you for having this conversation.

We do appreciate all you do for the children and want you to be part of their lives. I hope you understand why we need to have a sense of organization with our routines. It has to be about the children and they have to see us all trying to get along and being happy."

This agreement gave me a reprieve for a few years. The negative feelings I had towards Alice were still there, but not as pronounced. I often wondered how Alice felt. Would her feelings towards me subside or fester? Who knows? Controlling the environment with this agreement helped greatly.

Alice eventually developed a life of her own and married Sam. Tom always says that was the best day of his life!

Step Changes:
1. Become a better listener.
2. Learn to communicate with my spouse and children.
3. Consider counseling.

Chapter 7

The Arrival of James

My belly was getting bigger and bigger and I was ready to have this child. This baby would be a blessing. This was Tom's third time around having a baby and he was very calm during the whole pregnancy. I wanted him to be as excited as I was, since everything was new to me. I did not see the excitement in Tom, and I was hurt a little by his nonchalance regarding this pregnancy. I was reading everything I could get my hands on and wanted him to learn alongside me.

I wanted to know all about the changes in my body. What a miracle!

"Tom, The baby is about 10 inches long right now."

"Yes, Jo."

My emotions were wild, and I scolded him one morning.

"Tom, don't you want this baby? Why aren't you interested in what is happening to my body and how our child is growing?"

He grabbed my hands and said, "Forgive me, Jo. I will love our child, but there is so much more. I have to protect and support him or her. It is a big responsibility. A baby is a big commitment and I look at the practical side a little more than you do."

I understand that now. The memory of how much energy his children took when they were little was still fresh in his mind.

I continued to read every book I could get my hands on. Although I was a stepmother to two children at home, I had never experienced the baby years. I was idealistic about the whole idea of adding one more child to our household, but had some concerns as well.

Would Andrew and Sarah welcome this new child or would they be jealous?

It was frightening for me to consider all I had been through and how this life event could once again change the dynamics of our family. I was just getting to a point where I felt accepted.

One night I panicked and realized that we had not had a conversation with Alice regarding our new addition. I asked Tom if this would be a good idea.

"It isn't really anything she will be involved in," he said.

"Tom, could she sabotage the relationship between the siblings in any way?"

"Well, Jo I don't know. But if you want to have a conversation with her, that is fine with me."

"Tom, I want YOU to have the conversation with her. I want you to encourage her to allow the children to accept this child as their sister or brother. I don't want her alienating the children from their new sibling."

"Okay, Jo. I will talk to her."

And suddenly, I was ready to bring Tom Walden's third child into the world. He was a little boy, and we named him James Samuel Walden.

The next six months went by fairly quickly. By now, little James went to bed at 6:00 p.m. and slept until 6:00 a.m. Andrew and Sarah were beside themselves with joy. They loved their new brother, and I had been worried for nothing. Our family was the best it had been in a long time, and I realized all those labor pains were worth it.

After James was born, our household became a positive environment. I was able to stay home from work to take care of the baby, and that actually helped my relationship with Andrew and Sarah. I had more time to do things that would help them feel special, and they were able to spend time with James. They really began to love him.

It was during James' first year of life that I realized having three children was time consuming. I was up early every morning and exhausted by nightfall. Tom realized that I needed to quit work and stay home to raise our family. I agreed.

As James grew, our children grew closer and closer. And more importantly, I felt that Sarah and Andrew came to know me and love me a little more. It was the best feeling to have that happening in our family.

The years flew past, and at the age of five, it became evident that James was a lot like Tom. He followed his father around constantly.

James loved cars, and he loved going to work with his dad. He knew every make and model. Tom owned a Ford dealership and he and James each had their favorite makes and models. This made Tom happy, and he pulled up a child's desk next to his and let James put models together while he worked.

James didn't know it at the time, but he was being primed to take over the business one day.

Step Changes:
1. Counseling probably would have helped!

Chapter 8

The Teen Years: Andrew and Sarah

The years seemed to flow a little better. I gauged this by my relationship with Tom's children. If the kids were not on an even keel, the family wasn't either. In a stepfamily, whether children verbalize it or not, they almost always wish that their mother and father would get back together.

I believe:

It is okay for children of divorced parents to be sad when their parents separate.

It is okay for the biological parents to validate that feeling.

It is okay for the children to have a good relationship with the stepparent. This does not mean that they have to love the stepparent equally as they do their biological parent, and it is okay for the biological parent to validate those feelings.

It is okay that you love your mother or father more than me. I am okay with just being a friend.

Those words may help a lot of stepfamilies. It took me a lot of years to learn this.

Things were pretty good with the kids during these years. When I told Tom he had to handle something, he knew I meant it. When Tom handled the sticky situations, our lives did not become emotionally complicated. The situations happened and they got resolved, and our lives were so much better for several years.

I think moms and dads grow into parenting. In the beginning, the situations are simple and, as the child grows, the situations become more complex.

Little children/little problems, bigger children/bigger problems. There is some truth to that, I have found.

I have made many parenting mistakes, but I always truly had their best interests at heart, which is why I wanted to go to counseling! I wanted to make it work.

I worked so hard to try to earn Andrew and Sarah's love. Looking back, I think I did it all wrong. I wish I would have gone to counseling on my own. If I had just praised or acknowledged their accomplishments verbally, instead of bribing them with things, we might have developed better patterns of behavior. It was all so complicated. A new pair of shoes solved things quickly, for the moment. In the long run, it was disastrous. I should have done less and stepped back when situations got sticky. They came to expect things from me and I was not appreciated. I must say that Sarah really tried, as she got older, to accept me into her life as a parent and a friend.

The children occasionally still blamed me for things as the years went by, and it caused a lot of heartache in our family. I sometimes felt that the effort I put into our routines and daily activities was not appreciated, and nothing I did helped. I did not know how to help.

My fear was that James would see some of this negative behavior and model it. He watched their reactions to me and occasionally, he would come up to me after an incident and say, "Mommy, I still love you."

That reaction was very telling. As James grew older, instead of reacting to some of these situations, he just walked away or pretended it did not happen. He just did not want to deal with it.

James loved Andrew and Sarah. They were his brother and sister, and it was a simple as that. He grew up with them from his beginning, and he truly did not differentiate between a step and a biological sibling. They were his family.

As a family, we never discussed the conflicting feelings the children had for this step world. For each of us, they were different.

Andrew was afraid of losing his father's love.

James was afraid of losing his brother's and sister's love.

Sarah was the peacemaker in the family. She just wanted everyone to be happy. Her way of helping was to bake cookies. She found this put a smile on everyone's face, and she did it so often that after one argument, Andrew shouted, "Hey, Sarah! I want chocolate chip this time."

The situation with Andrew became a little more manageable, and I hoped that someday Andrew would come to understand the dynamics and see the value of our stepfamily. It was an ongoing struggle. I slowly disconnected from Andrew, and I'm sorry to say that this helped me immensely. The more removed I was from his situations, the better we got along. Heaven forbid I would comment on anything he did, because whatever I said was wrong.

It was the only way I could keep my emotional being in check. I realized that our relationship would always be stressed.

Things did not go as well as I hoped during these important years for Andrew and Sarah. Dealing with hormones and puberty were many of the reasons for our struggles, but they were compounded by this step crazy situation. We all needed professional guidance from a counselor, and none of us got it.

As long as I was giving Andrew the material things he wanted, he was decent. Sarah was better, but a new dress or new shoes always helped her attitude.

The sad thing about this is, at times I ignored my own child and his needs to make sure that my stepchildren were on an even keel. I knew my biological son would still know I loved him, even if he got the short end of the stick.

Feelings are so complicated and many times you learn without any words being said. You just understand the situation. I just wish my learning would have happened before the struggles occurred.

Step Changes:
1. COUNSELING!

Chapter 9

Sarah

Sarah grew into a young woman very quickly, and her father missed the change. He always looked at her like she was still a little girl. Many fathers do that, and then one day it hits them. Pow! Their little girl is all grown up.

As the years passed, Sarah and I continued to have a good relationship. At times it was a little bumpy, but we always managed to get through it and come out friends, which is more than I can say about my relationship with Andrew.

When I first married Tom, I thought that if I had any trouble with his children, it would be with Sarah. The bond between a father and daughter is strong, and I thought she might become jealous. I was also concerned about Alice, because sometimes mothers try to cling to their daughters. I was afraid of this step relationship, and I think I was a little hesitant in dealing with Sarah. That hesitancy might have been the saving grace in our relationship.

When Sarah was in High School, she started to notice boys. She was very pretty and they were calling all the time. This worried me, as I had come to think of Sarah as my own. I wanted to protect her from any teenage trauma and I told this to my husband on many occasions. He reminded me that experiences help you grow up. Sarah would make mistakes but she would learn from them. He said children have to be grounded in good teachings and eventually they will be fine. I wish it was that simple!

When Sarah turned 16, things immediately got worse. One evening Sarah brought home a boyfriend. His name was Ray, and he was the town football hero. The problem was that he was a senior, two years older than Sarah. She had a major crush on him.

I watched their interactions closely. Tom felt sure they were not having sex.

I was not so sure. They were constantly touching each other and looked very comfortable doing just that.

Sarah sensed my dislike for her boyfriend, and I knew it would affect our relationship. I tried to keep quiet, but I was so afraid she would get hurt by this boyfriend, and I wanted to protect her from him.

As the weeks went on, Sarah continued to date Ray with Tom's blessing.

One evening after one of Ray's football games, we had a situation.

I heard a noise coming from one of the kids' rooms. It was 1:00 a.m. and I was concerned for their safety. Andrew was away at college and James was sound asleep. Nothing ever woke James up.

I got up to see what the noise was, and saw that the window in Sarah's bedroom was propped open with a book and Sarah was not in bed.

I looked out the window in time to see Sarah and Ray running across the yard beside the house.

Not having sex? Sure. I had no idea what to do, but I thought about it and realized that, as a stepparent, I could not be the one to find this situation. The consequences would be too great for my family. So, I went back to my room and crawled in bed.

I know that sometimes you have to take the brunt of things even if the children hate you for it, but I was not willing to break Tom's heart over this. After a minute or so, I nudged Tom and said, "Get up! I heard something from one of the kids' rooms. Please check them."

He got up, saw the open window, and came back to the room with phone in hand. He was reporting his daughter missing. The police came to the house to take a report and, shortly thereafter, Sarah came walking up the driveway. He hugged her and let her flimsy explanation slide, but the next day he had a security system installed.

About a year later, I had suspicions that Sarah was having sex with another boyfriend. I tried to talk to Tom about this. He would not believe it.

To be a parent is to be watchful, be involved, know the other parents, and be where your child is, knowing every step they make along the way. Yes, as parents, we occasionally misstep. But I think in a way we are supposed to miss some things. These are the growing up events that make our children adults.

After my conversation with Tom regarding this new boyfriend, I realized I had to handle this myself. I knew it could potentially turn on me if I became involved. Alice would certainly blame me, and Tom would never believe that his daughter would have sex with her boyfriend. But for Sarah's sake, I had to take the risk. I decided to go to my gynecologist and ask her advice.

Fortunately, we lived in a small town outside of Annapolis, MD. The doctor was a friend of mine and knew our family situation. She listened to my concerns and finally said, "I am going to give you a three-month supply of birth control pills for Sarah. I expect her to come and see me for an appointment within those three months. And Jo," she said firmly, "I cannot tell you if she comes in, so don't ask me. You are opening the door for her and that is all you can do."

I went home that evening, and Sarah asked me to take her shopping for a dress. Her new boyfriend had asked her to the Christmas Ball.

Perfect, I thought.

I was unsure about how to approach the subject. Should I give her a book to read about getting pregnant? NO! She was smart and a teenager. Kids know everything today.

Should I start by asking her if she was having sex? I did not like that option either. I finally decided that the less said, the better. I did not want it to sound like I was trying to be involved in her personal relationship. So, I put the pills in a small box, along with the card from the doctor so she could call her for a follow up appointment.

The shopping trip started out well. We went to several shops and finally Sarah found the perfect dress. I knew I should approach the subject after we bought the dress, and little did Sarah know that she could have had any dress she wanted that night.

I wanted her to have the best attitude possible for listening to what I had to say. I knew if we had any argument at all, or if I said, "No, find a dress that is not that expensive," she would not listen to me. Sometimes, that's just the way kids are, step or not!

After she found her dress, I offered to take her to her favorite restaurant for something to eat. She liked that idea!

After we ordered, I said, "Sarah, I want to give you something. I will preface this gift by saying you can do anything you want with it after I give it to you, but I want you to know that I have come to love you as my own and I want to help guide you in any way I can. I want to encourage you to make good decisions in life and go on to college, graduate, and fulfill your dreams. I don't want anything to hinder those goals."

Sarah looked at me very strangely. I handed her a box with the pills and the doctor's card inside, with a note stating that she was to set up an appointment.

I quickly said, "Maybe you don't need them now, but you might in the future. Please don't throw them away. Now let's eat. No more discussion."

She got up from her chair, and I was afraid she was going to walk out of the restaurant. I thought to myself, "I just blew it! Why didn't I stay out of this?"

But then she came around the table and gave me a hug. I had tears in my eyes. I was a ball of nerves. I never knew what happened with the pills or the appointment, but Sarah never got pregnant.

Sarah graduated from high school and went on to college in Washington, DC. She and that boyfriend broke up shortly after her freshman year in college.

I am very proud of Sarah, and proud I had the sense to do what I did. As a stepparent, you have to pick your situations carefully — you know, the ones you have to get involved in. It is tricky!

This is a good example of the difference between handling a "step situation" and a "biological situation" with a child. If Sarah had been my own daughter, I would have owned the situation by sitting her down and talking with her. At least I hope I would have done that. Then I would have scheduled the appointment! It's just not that easy in a step environment! One must tread lightly.

There has to be a sense of respect and trust between the stepparent and stepchild. This takes time to develop and is not easy. I feel successful as a stepmother to Sarah knowing that she accepted my advice. I hope in the future, when she has her own children, she will remember that day and be able to make tough decisions regarding her own children.

Step Changes:
1. Counseling.

CHAPTER 10

James, My Biological Son, Why Do I Describe Him That Way?

There is a difference in raising a stepchild and a biological child. A big difference! A parent must tread very carefully and completely analyze every possible outcome when dealing with a stepchild.

Should I talk to her father?
Should I talk to her mother?
How should I say it?
When do I say it?

I have talked with many stepparents who have had this experience.

With a biological child, things are pretty easy, although a step-sibling can have an effect on the biological child. At times, they can become very jealous of the parent's feelings for their step-sibling or vice versa.

Things were pretty benign when James was in elementary and middle school. He idolized his brother and sister, always wanting to be and do whatever they were doing. He would sit and watch their soccer and swim practices. He was very proud of them, and they adored him, too. It seemed like a healthy sibling relationship.

Then James entered high school. He was a handsome boy, about 5 feet 11 inches tall in the ninth grade and well-built for his age. He had brown hair and brown eyes. He looked a lot like me, although he definitely had Tom's personality. He had his work ethic and love of business.

One Sunday afternoon, when James was 15, Tom came home with a new car. It was a midnight blue, Ford Mustang two-door. James was beside himself, because this was his favorite car. He didn't say anything, but he was hoping it was for him. It was not James' birthday, so what was Tom thinking?

We had the whole family coming for dinner that night, and I realized Tom was going to have to explain the car, and why he did not get one for Sarah or Andrew when they were 15.

Tom could not help but notice the excitement in James' eyes. James was chomping at the bit to drive it. He had just received his learner's permit the month before. Tom threw James the keys and away they went. I was not privy to their conversation, and found myself wondering in what way I would be blamed or shunned because James got a car. I pondered every possible outcome, and was a nervous wreck.

When Andrew turned 16, his father gave him a used Chevy four-door. It was nice, but it was not sporty. Tom held the keys at all times. Andrew had to ask his father when he wanted to drive it, and he seemed to be okay with that at the time. How would he react when he saw what Tom had done for James?

In many families, the youngest child often gets the nicest car when he or she turns 16. That is usually because when the oldest child turned 16, the parents didn't have enough money to buy a nicer car. That is just the way it works in a biological family.

But in this case, Andrew could view the situation in one of two ways:

When Andrew was 16, Tom could not afford to buy him a brand new car.

Tom loved James more than Andrew.

Tom didn't love James any more than he loved Andrew, but Andrew was always striving for Tom's attention. Would Andrew understand that Tom did not love James more than he loved him?

When Sarah turned 16, her father did not think she was interested in cars. He let her use the family car instead of giving her a car. And he was right — she didn't care at all. So I thought Sarah would be okay with the situation. But I was pretty sure Andrew would be upset. I have learned a little over the years.

Andrew and Sarah were due for dinner shortly. My strategy was to stay in the kitchen preparing the meal.

Sarah was first. "Wow, whose car is in the driveway?" she asked.

I replied, "I'm not sure. Maybe it's a loaner from the dealership. Go ask your dad."

No more discussion from her. She could have cared less beyond the first comment. Sarah was never into cars much, and she had no need for a car as she was not allowed to have one at college her freshman year. No problems on her end!

Next was Andrew. Now, let me preface this with the fact that Andrew was 28 years old. He did not want to go into the family business. He saw his father work the long hours and decided he wanted to be an accountant. Tom was disappointed, but he understood.

Andrew walked through the door and did not say a word. Not one word. James ran up to his brother and said, "Come see our new car!"

I assumed when I heard this that Tom had not told James the car was his. Good move!

Andrew said, "No thanks. I'll see it when I leave."

James was deflated. He just looked at Andrew in disbelief. Then it started.

Andrew said, "Where is Dad?" I pointed to the pool area, where his dad was grilling dinner. Andrew walked out there and started to grill Tom.

"Gee, Dad, I see you bought James a car, and he's not even 16."

"No, I didn't buy him a car. It is my car and, if he gets good grades and works hard, he will be able to drive it with my permission."

Then Andrew said, "You never did anything like that for me."

Tom responded, "Andrew, I never had the money to do that for you. And I did buy you a car! Things are better for us now."

Andrew quickly responded, "You mean better for you and Josie. Not you and Mom."

Tom looked at Andrew and said, "Andrew you are too old to be acting like this. Please do not spoil this evening for our family."

"I am not spoiling the evening for us, Dad. You spoiled our life! You married your girlfriend! What were you thinking? Of course, you have James, and now he gets everything! You don't even care about us or Mom. I have had it! I am out of here."

Tom tried to talk to him. "Andrew, let's sit down and talk. I can see you are upset. I love you and your sister dearly and I did love your mother, but we could not live together and we divorced. It was mutual."

James heard the whole conversation, and said, "Andrew, the car is not mine. Please don't be mad at me. Why do you wish they never had me? You are not being fair."

Sarah was disgusted with his comments. "Oh, Andrew. Grow up!"

Andrew was still angry. This could possibly be the end of my relationship with Andrew forever. And I wasn't even involved. No amount of money would suffice this time. I just kept playing it cool, acting as if I did not hear any of the conversation.

Andrew would not let his dad explain. He just stormed through the house, out the door, and went home. When Tom came in, I asked, "Where did Andrew go? Did he forget something?" Tom said, "No, he didn't."

Tom did not comment any further, but this type of situation is where children can make their parents feel really guilty they got divorced. Tom sat down and put his head in his hands. Tom's father finished the grilling, and we all pretended to have a nice meal.

James forgot that Andrew stormed off, and Sarah was embarrassed by her brother's actions, but she didn't say anything. She tried to make up for him by being overly kind to her dad and James.

The smartest thing I ever did was to stay completely out of that situation.

One week went by, and still no sign of Andrew. James called him and, of course, he did not answer the phone. I heard James leave a message that said, "Andrew, the car is not mine. It's Dad's. Please don't hate me."

Andrew refused to come to the house from that point on. I think he felt a little guilty regarding James, because he did call a few weeks later and offer to take James out to a movie so he could spend time with him.

Eventually, Andrew went to his dad's work and tried to act as if nothing was bothering him. But he didn't come to our house again for a year, and that was because he blamed me. Oh, the craziness of it all.

The only good thing about the car situation was that Andrew could not say one word to me about what occurred because I was not involved. But somehow I became the scapegoat. It didn't hurt as much that time, because I wasn't involved and it was clear to me that I shouldn't feel bad.

Tom was affected big time. He was getting a taste of what I had gone through all those years.

As James grew, the relationship between him and Andrew eased a little. Tom tried to stay out of it. He would say it was a life lesson. Tom never believed in spending equally on the kids at Christmas. He felt if one needed something and he could afford to help them, he did. He felt they were all at different stages in their lives, and they would all get their turn at some point.

Step Changes:
1. Communicate with the children and be proactive.
2. Counseling. We would have learned this in counseling!

Chapter 11

Step Friends

*I*n the step crazy world, there is another aspect that has to be addressed. That is step friends. In many situations, a couple not only divorces each other, but they have to divorce their friends, church, etc.

This creeps up on you slowly. I did not have a clue that we would have problems in this arena. It never even crossed my mind.

When a divorce is final, friends have to make a decision. They have to choose a side. Sometimes it takes years before friends get back together again, if they ever do. Sometimes the friends never really know what happened in the split between their companions.

Sometimes it is easy for the step friends to choose. If they're neighbors, then it's easy, because whoever gets the house gets the friends. Or at least it seems to work that way. Any way it goes, it is a tough time emotionally for all involved.

The friends know the 4th of July parties will never be the same, and the Christmas Eve parties will be at someone else's house. If you live in a small town, you are screwed. But if you live in a city, it is easy to avoid the situation, which is usually unspoken. Come on now, wouldn't it be easier just to discuss these things?

If your kids hang out with your friends' kids, you are really in trouble. Not an easy situation for all involved! In our situation, it was bad.

Tom said to me one night, early in our relationship, "Jo, our relationship has grown and I know I should have explained to the kids that you are more than a friend by now. There is one more reason I have kept things under wraps, and that is my ex-wife. She can be very possessive, and I'm not sure how she will react. That is why I wanted the kids to get to know you as a friend first. I do not want to risk anyone influencing them in a negative way."

"I think it is probably time to tell them, because several of your friends realize that we are a couple, and I would hate for your children to hear it from them and not you." He agreed.

I was new to all of this, and I did not have the other life. I knew deep down that I loved Tom and I was excited to start a new life. I realized pretty quickly that my new life had to be his current life, if that makes sense.

I don't think Tom wanted to divorce everything in his ex-life. He couldn't because of his children. He could not ask them to move, or to get new friends. He also had a business that depended on the public, and long-time friends in the area.

I was the one who had to adapt to the children, friends, church, teachers, etc. There was only going to be one change for Tom, and that was a new wife in his old house.

Tom called after he put the kids to bed. He told me the conversation went really well. He said the children were okay with us dating, and that they liked me. Although he said they did ask him if we were going to get married, and if they would have to get a new house and new friends. Tom assured them that we were just dating and nothing would change in their lives. So all was well, and the kids seemed to be okay with our relationship.

A few days later Alice started to quiz the children about us. It was the weekend, and Andrew bounced in the door just as we returned from dinner. A neighbor brought him home from football practice.

He looked at his dad and said, "Dad, Mom asked me if I knew you had a new girlfriend. I said I already knew. Sarah forgot, but I reminded her. I told Mom we were the first to know."

Tom and I chuckled a little when he left the room. Maybe things would go a little easier than we thought.

I started to invite a few of my friends over for dinner occasionally. This worked, and Tom enjoyed himself. We slowly started to develop a new social life. Tom's old friends seldom called anymore, and it was evident they had not chosen Tom.

We still saw a few friends of theirs, but it was evident that we felt more comfortable with our own group, one that did not have a history.

Some of Tom and Alice's friends continued to ask us to gatherings, but this was hard because we usually saw Alice there. Occasionally, it would be a small group and Alice was not there.

We did not expect this change in our life or in Tom's circle of friends. It just happened. Every aspect of life is affected when a couple goes through a divorce.

Step Changes:
1. Talk with your ex-spouse and decide how you are going to tell your friends about your divorce.
2. Counseling. Of course, you would learn this and how to do it in counseling.

CHAPTER 12

Holidays

WOW! Holidays can get really hairy. The first few were the toughest for our children. They had to figure out who they should buy presents for, how much was okay to spend on me, and whether they would even tell Alice that they bought a present for me.

This was really complicated. They didn't want to offend anyone, specifically their mother. Their mother didn't have a boyfriend yet, and she would tell them how lonely she was, so they always saw her as the victim in our family picture. The first holiday was really scary for the kids.

One day I heard Andrew on the phone talking to his grandmother, and he said, "Grandma, when Dad married Josie, all the rules changed."

That statement said so much.

Of course, Tom and I were planning our activities for the holiday and we thought we were creating some great activities. We thought the children would enjoy them. Did we even think to ask the kids what they wanted? No. Big mistake! The kids were mad and no one knew why!

Everyone in our household seemed sad, and it just wasn't right. We tried to cheer up the kids, but they were young and did not or could not express their feelings. We did not even know the reason they were cranky. They just acted out. I'm not even sure they knew why they were upset. We would get upset with them and tell them to change their attitudes, and everyone was sad. Then we realized the kids were upset that the holiday activities had changed. They were not what they used to be.

We unknowingly did this to our children, even though we had their best interests at heart. We didn't know how to communicate with them so they understood what was happening in their lives. It had to be confusing for them.

It was sad, and we spent the first Christmas agonizing over what we did wrong. Of course, if we had gone to counseling, I think we could have headed off this problem, or at least handled it a little differently.

Counseling, please!

Holidays take their toll on families without the introduction of a step environment. When I think back, we did the best we could. We tried to create a comfortable, emotionally healthy, safe environment. So, I guess it could have been worse.

Biological parents have their own stumbling blocks, but everyone seems to deal with the same struggles and those struggles are acceptable. The parents talk about their situations willingly.

For some reason, stepfamilies tend to keep their struggles to themselves. Maybe it's embarrassment that we can't handle it, or maybe we are just embarrassed that our marriages failed. Who knows?

Step Changes:
1. You know the answer. COUNSELING!

Chapter 13

That is not your seat!
Don't touch my things!
She is not my sister!
He is not my brother!
I hate you!

Oh my! I don't know how the children survived their father's divorce. I could barely maintain normalcy, and I wasn't even part of it. I was an adult, and I could talk to friends about my situation. The children didn't have anyone objective to talk to or any way to process it. How did they do it?

Was it the routine? Maybe.

Was it friends? Maybe.

When I look back, I see the many mistakes that I made in dealing with my stepchildren. There is nothing I can do now. I used to think that demonstrating my love for their father would show them that true love makes families happier. Was it showing them instead that their mother was not part of this family and was sad and not in their lives anymore?

Who knows?

Did their mother alienate them from me in any way, or did the children just sense an unspoken loss? Were they mourning the loss of what they knew as their family? When all Sarah and Andrew saw was their mother did not like me, it was pretty easy for them to decide that they should not like me. It did not matter how much their father liked me.

I will say it did help a little when Alice met Sam. Once Alice was happy, the kids did not have to defend her so much. Children want to see their mom and dad happy!

The step world is a confusing world to children. Do you alternate holidays? Do you alternate weekends and take the kids out of their familiar rooms? What is the best way to help the kids deal with a divorce without leaving them scarred?

Andrew has a wife of his own now, and I pray they never get divorced.

Sarah has a boyfriend, although nothing serious, I hope.

And James does not seem to be affected by any of this. What does that tell you? James comes home for every holiday. He does not have to split his time with his father's family or his mother's family. He does not have to compete for either parents love with a new stepmother or stepfather. If I had it to do all over again, I would have insisted on counseling for all of us!

If Tom had to do it over again, I am not sure what he would do. Would he even get married a second time knowing how it would affect his children?

Who knows?

It was a struggle all those years!

I tried my best and I know Tom did, too. I do believe that for many years I sacrificed my attention and love for my own son, because I was trying to gain the love of my stepchildren. Does my biological son resent me for that?

As a stepparent I went overboard with my stepchildren, because I thought it would help. I did not have to do that for my biological child, because Mom and Dad were all he had. One set of parents, one family holiday. Everything seemed normal.

I beat myself up all the time by thinking about this. In fact I think I have lost years of my life because of the stress. My husband and I often talk about this. Everything we ever did, whether right or wrong, was for our children. Someday all of them, biological and step, will realize how much we love them.

Now that they are all out of the house, Tom and I are somewhat stress free.

Maybe we can get some of those years back.

Chapter 14

It's Our Turn

Andrew and Amy were leaving for their honeymoon. They looked so happy as they got in the limousine to leave. When they return, they will live about 30 minutes from us.

Sarah has her own apartment and is a buyer for a large department store. She graduated from college with a business degree. I don't think Tom and Alice's divorce ever affected her negatively. She seems to be just fine.

James is in college, and is getting a degree in business management. He wants to own a car dealership one day. Imagine that!

Tom and I will be celebrating our anniversary in February. As I am thinking about all this, I am curled up in Tom's strong arms. He looks at me and says, "How about going to Montreal, Canada for our anniversary?"

I respond, "Sounds like a plan!"

www.ingramcontent.com/pod-product-compliance
Lightning Source LLC
Chambersburg PA
CBHW022108040426
42451CB00007B/172